*   *   *   D0139621

Writing well, and persuasively, is a discipline that can be learned. This book introduces the essential skills, rules, and steps for producing effective political prose—from the editorial, the op-ed, and the polemical essay to other forms both weighty and seemingly slight. Drafting commission reports, policy memoranda, and press releases requires skill. Writing speeches or ghosting essays for a principal calls upon special sensitivities. Blogging is best done with discipline. There are rules for ceremonial remarks, letters, and toasts.

Author Adam Garfinkle, founding editor of *The American Interest*, has long experience as a successful political wordsmith in many venues. He developed a course in political writing for interns working in government and think tank offices in Washington, DC. This book makes that course, along with a sprinkling of the author's trademark wit and wisdom, widely available.

*   *   *

POLITICAL WRITING

A Guide to the Essentials

Adam Garfinkle

With a foreword by David Brooks

M.E.Sharpe
Armonk, New York
London, England

Library of Congress Cataloging-in-Publication Data

Garfinkle, Adam M., 1951–
  Political writing : a guide to the essentials / by Adam Garfinkle.
    p. cm.
  ISBN 978-0-7656-3123-7 (hardcover : alk. paper); ISBN 978-0-7656-3124-4 (pbk. : alk. paper)
  1. Rhetoric—Political aspects. 2. Speechwriting. 3. Government report writing. 4. Political
letter writing. 5. Political science—Authorship. I. Title.

  P301.5.P67G37 2012
  808.06′623—dc23   2011049952

Printed in the United States of America

The paper used in this publication meets the minimum requirements of
American National Standard for Information Sciences
Permanence of Paper for Printed Library Materials,
ANSI Z 39.48-1984.

♾

IBT (c) 10   9   8   7   6   5   4   3   2   1
SP (p)   10   9   8   7   6   5   4   3   2   1

This book is dedicated to Harvey Sicherman:
friend, colleague, mentor, and man of style.

CONTENTS

FOREWORD

I might as well tell you right now that this little book is going to shake your self-confidence. In these pages, Adam Garfinkle holds up a standard of excellence for how to think, argue, and be that very few of us can match. Again and again I found myself underlining passages and thinking to myself, "Yes, I really should do that." This pertained to advice not only on how to present an argument and write a column, but on how to be a serious person—how to put aside the trivialities and distractions of life—yes, I'm talking to you, Twitter—and build up knowledge and wisdom.

He also reminds us why most educational systems in most ages put rhetoric at the very heart of schooling. We spend much of our lives trying to organize our views of reality and then trying to persuade other people to share them. It is very important to understand these crafts.

Most of the emphasis these days is placed on the "persuading people" part of that activity, but here I want to dwell on the other part: "organizing our views of reality." That is the most important part of the art of rhetoric. As Garfinkle notes in these pages, it actually is very rare that we can change somebody's mind about an issue. What we are sometimes able to do, however, is to get someone to see the world in a new way, and that new way of seeing necessarily leads them to new ways of acting.

Let me tell you about something that happened to me as I was reading Garfinkle's book. I was working on a column on fiscal policy and a debate between President Barack Obama and Republican Representative Paul Ryan about their competing views. I interviewed a few White House officials. I interviewed Ryan and a few congressional budget mavens. I printed out and read studies from the Congressional Budget Office, the Tax Policy Center, the Committee for a Responsible Federal Budget, and other wonk outfits.

By the time I was done with my research, I had about 400 pages of notes and studies, and five entirely contradictory sets of data. My job as a columnist is to try to come up with one coherent narrative to help people understand all these claims and counterclaims. My job is to give my readers a frame through which to see this debate. The basic thesis I came up with is this: Ryan's plan is seriously flawed, but it at least points us toward fiscal balance. Obama's criticisms of it are valid, but his own plans don't do enough to reduce debt. Obama wants to preserve some good programs, while Ryan aims to avoid a fiscal catastrophe.

The day the column appeared I received three furious calls from the White House saying I had not been fair to their plans and two angry emails from Republicans saying that I had not been fair to their plans and I had been too kind to Obama.

It would be easy to say, "Well, if I am offending both sides then I must have it right." But Garfinkle's book is a cure for that sort of smugness and complacency. It sends a core message that you have to respect the craft you are trying to perform and understand how others have truly excelled in performing it. In the frame of mind inspired by this short manual, I have to admit that both sides made some compelling criticisms of my column: I did not describe reality entirely accurately. I am going to have to write a few more columns to stumble toward a more supple depiction of reality.

So much of good writing and good living is having a lofty set of standards by which to judge yourself.

And now I would like to use these last paragraphs to offer a little advice of my own.

First, know that by the time you sit down at the keyboard, your work should be 80 percent done. Writing is about traffic management—organization. I think geographically, so I have to physically organize my writing on the floor of my basement. I take all my notes and I organize them in piles in a row across the floor. Each pile represents a paragraph of my column. Before I start writing I may have a dozen or more piles stretched across the floor. Then I pick up a pile of notes, write the paragraph, and move on to the next pile.

Sometimes, in the middle of the writing process, I find that my organizational frame does not work and my argument is not flowing. Judges have a great saying for this: The opinion won't write. When that happens, I have to start over and come up with another way to organize my piles. The pile-making is the biggest part of the writing process.

The other piece of advice is to find a simple, natural voice. To understand what I mean, read George Orwell, Robert Benchley, or C.S. Lewis. Garfinkle has some great reading selections in this book, but Orwell and Lewis are the masters of simple, natural prose. Their styles told you there was a great personality behind the writing—and that is an essential part of persuasion.

In the world of the new media, some of Garfinkle's advice may seem old school, but if you absorb the wisdom that he has distilled in this little book, it will help you to have a much bigger impact on this world.

—David Brooks

David Brooks is a columnist for the *New York Times* and commentator on *PBS NewsHour.*

INTRODUCTION
How This Book Came to Be

Once upon a time I invented and taught a course in political writing at the University of California's Washington, DC–based academic internship program (UCDC). After teaching the course several times and having had scores of students ask for my notes or other ways to better remember my lectures, I finally agreed to turn my course preparations into a small book. The result is the volume you see before you now.

Like the class, this book is about political writing as a subset of writing in general, which can serve many purposes other than persuasion. But political writing in all its forms is fundamentally about persuasion or, at the least, the management of impressions. Whether someone changes your mind and you know it, or manages to influence you in ways you cannot detect, you are persuaded either way—and, as a result, you may act differently than you would have otherwise.

The pages that follow teach the "dark arts" of persuasion and impression management on various levels. After several decades of uncertainty, I have concluded that writing on the level of a fine art cannot be taught, though it can be learned.[1] Writing devoted to political persuasion does not meet the definition of a fine art. It is not done for its own sake or for the sake of its inherent beauty as with other artistic forms. It serves a less elevated, though not necessarily ignoble, purpose: to make waves in the real world of policy, either directly or indirectly, by affecting the intellectual milieu in which policy is made. These skills can be learned. Whether they can also be taught to anyone in particular, however, depends as much on the student as on the teacher.

---

1. I concur with Joseph Epstein in "Heavy Sentences," *The New Criterion* (June 2011).

Following the logic and sequence of my political writing class, the lessons in this slim volume begin in Chapter 1 with an attempt to impart some general understanding of the nature of *rhetoric* and *polemic*. Only after this foundation has been established can we proceed effectively to the how-to phase of writing for a political purpose. When we reach the practical instruction stage in the text, we go in sequence from basic exercises covering how to write (Chapters 2 and 3) to the particular forms of persuasive writing: from essays to reviews, op-eds, speeches, memoranda, and other manifestations of the craft (Chapters 4 through 12).

The only topic raised in this book but not included in the class is the penultimate one, on blogging. I have added this chapter at the wise request of the publisher, but I did not initially accept the idea in loving embrace. This is because I regard blogging as part of an invidious cultural trend that, at least as of 2012, contributes to the evisceration of logical standards in the discussion of political and social ideas. But life being what it is these days, I have accepted the call to try to help others make the best of the form, as I have tried in my own occasional blogging to do for myself.

This book differs from my university course in four ways. First, a course presupposes a social interaction in which students engage with one another as well as with their teacher. The emotional power of classroom interaction is a natural and necessary part of the educational process, and don't let anyone tell you otherwise. You can't get that kind of engagement from any book, which a reader typically eyes in a sedate and solipsistic manner. (Look around you now to take stock of your surroundings. Are you alone for all practical purposes? Is the place where you are sitting or lying recumbent reasonably quiet? I thought so.)

Second, my political writing course included assigned readings and other preparatory activities to help students understand lectures and generate better questions for discussion. Nearly all of these readings had a dual purpose: to show students examples of good (and not-so-good) political writing; and to impart knowledge from the substance of their subjects, all of it about politics of one sort or another—from international to national to local.

It is not practical for legal and logistical reasons for me to include in this book the many readings I assigned, or to expect all my readers to find and study that material on their own. Nevertheless, I have placed boxes at the end of each chapter listing relevant readings and an occasional reference, and I have offered what I think are useful writing exercises. I have kept the reading lists modest—much shorter than those assigned to my classes—in the expectation that shorter lists are more likely to be actually engaged than longer ones. Most of the readings are readily available on the internet, and the titles in each chapter's "Recommended Reading" box are listed in the order in which they are mentioned in the text.

You would be wise to access and familiarize yourself with as much of this pertinent reference material as possible as you study each chapter. Even better, you might familiarize yourself with relevant materials *before* reading a given chapter. If you happen to learn something from the political substance of these readings over and above learning from them as models of effective writing, so much the better. Attempting the writing assignments would do you no harm, either. Of course, I cannot make you do any of this and I will not be grading you, so you will incur no literal penalty for ignoring my advice—thus, my choice of the word *wise* above. No one can make anyone wise; wisdom is a quality of mind that must be earned.

Third, I taught my political writing courses in Washington, DC, where students were engaged in a rigorous internship program either on the Hill, in an Executive Branch agency, or in some think tank, professional association, or other advocacy outfit. My students and I dubbed the latter third of our weekly three-hour class "the Washington hour," during which the arts of persuasion merged with what students were experiencing at their internships, what was in the national and international news that week, and what emerged when their observations were sharpened by any insights I could offer. For all I know, you may be reading this book in Portland or Pago Pago. Alas, your location somewhere other than Washington cannot be helped.

Fourth, the classroom methodology forced students to write and rewrite, and to write and rewrite yet again, far more intensively than most were accustomed to doing. Each time we met as a group, students had to prepare a piece of writing based on the week's readings; I would then select one at random to edit on the classroom whiteboard. This writing clinic instructed students on a variety of topics as they arose—grammar, usage, punctuation and capitalization conventions, how to structure quotations, and so on, as well as the finer points of persuasive diction. (We devote Chapters 2 and 3 to just these sorts of general instruction that underlie the process of learning to write persuasively.) Students whose papers went under the editing knife in any given week tended to pay close attention to what was being done to their papers, as did students who sought to avoid gratuitous embarrassment in weeks to come.

After class, all students revised their papers in light of what had been learned during that session, and every writing assignment was revised yet again, and again as time allowed, until the entire semester file of writing was accumulated and handed in at the end of the term, suitably introduced and concluded. In addition, every student had a "buddy" with whom to share critical scrutiny, so that each one not only wrote a great deal but also learned to edit the works of others and assimilate into their own work the comments of peers.

Obviously, I cannot make readers whose names I do not know and whose faces I have never looked upon engage in this kind of rigorous process. I literally cannot make you spill one drop of ink or touch even one key on a keyboard if you are not so inclined. And even if you do attempt the writing assignments spelled out here, I will neither know nor be able to provide any constructive critique. But, of course, if this book is used in a classroom setting, all of these benefits can be restored to the educational process, and I encourage instructors who use this book in their writing classes to consider using my basic methodology for their own efforts. That kind of setting, I remain convinced, is the one from which the best uses of this volume can be made.

Given the extreme rarity of courses on rhetoric these days—a matter we will take up in Chapter 1—it may be that the best you will be able to do is to find yourself a "buddy" with whom to read and discuss this little book in tandem. While it is not always true that two heads are better than one—just ask any recovering schizophrenic—it is certainly true in this case.

This book is indeed *little* because I have tried to keep it both simple and concise. Some of the following chapters are only a few pages long, because that's all the space I needed to express my points on those subjects. I have also kept my tone conversational, using the second-person pronoun ("you," valued reader) to help the medicine go down a bit more smoothly (and a bit less formally).

One of the things you *must* learn in your quest to become a better writer is that all kinds of writing need to know certain limits; in other words, effective writing depends on *principles of exclusion*. It is not enough to know what you want to say, hard as that can be to figure out. It is equally important to identify what you will *not* try to say in any given effort. I have struggled to find principles of exclusion for this book in order to keep it short and user friendly. I certainly feel obligated to obey my own maxim that, when it comes to writing, less is more (and, of course, more is usually less). In cases in which I doubted whether a particular piece of advice was really necessary to achieve my purpose, I sometimes compromised by putting it into a footnote. More on the various uses of footnotes anon.

When I introduced my political writing course to students at our first class meeting, I felt obliged to disclose something about my qualifications to teach it. Someone, after all, was paying a lot of money for students to attend UCDC, so I figured I owed them full professorial disclosure. You (or someone else) paid much less to get your hands on this book, but I owe readers no less, for this reason: I respected the students who took my class because they constituted a minority who understood the importance of learning to write well; I respect you for what I presume to be your similar determination to work hard to improve your writing skills. So here goes.

I was born in Washington, DC and raised in the Washington metropolitan area. Neither of my parents worked for the U.S. government after I was born, but many of our neighbors did. It is hard to avoid the local political air around here if you are paying any attention at all. At a young age, I learned the truth of the quip that Washington is the only city in the world where sound travels faster than light. If you don't know what that means now, you will by the time you finish reading this book.

After public high school, I went off to the University of Pennsylvania in Philadelphia to study history and social science. I ended up staying at Penn for both undergraduate and graduate school, earning my Ph.D. in 1979. I worked for a think tank in Philadelphia while in graduate school and continued there after obtaining my doctorate. In addition, I worked "on loan" for a time in the U.S. Senate on strategic arms control issues. I also did adjunct teaching at Penn, Haverford College, Temple, and other institutions of higher learning.

All the while, I was writing reports, essays, and op-eds. I also wrote many memos as a think tank member and at least a few as a Senate staffer. While honing my writing skills, I had the good counsel of several colleagues; some of that counsel focused hard on the skills of political writing. Of those who mentored me, one man stands out above all others: Dr. Harvey Sicherman, to whom I have dedicated this book. So extraordinary were his skills at political writing that he went on to become a close aide and wordsmith for not one, but three U.S. Secretaries of State, a Secretary of the Navy, and other key political figures.

I also wrote a few books, among them *Telltale Hearts: The Origins and Impact of the Vietnam Antiwar Movement,* which was named a notable book of the year by the *New York Times Book Review.* Just as that book appeared, I entered the magazine business as executive editor of *The National Interest*, based in Washington, DC. There I worked for and with a true genius of a man, a Welshman via Australia named Owen Harries (whose wisdom we will tap more or less directly in Chapter 4). Additionally, I took up adjunct teaching at the School of Advanced International Studies (SAIS) of Johns Hopkins University. As I was learning the extent to which editing the works of others under the guidance of a master can improve one's own writing, I learned from my students that skillful communication is inherently a two-way relationship, as is true education itself.

After nearly four years of this apprenticeship, I joined the research staff of the U.S. Commission on National Security/21st Century, a federal commission known more commonly then and since as the Hart-Rudman Commission, after its two cochairs, former U.S. Senators Gary Hart and Warren Rudman. I was the chief writer for all three of the commission's reports, as well as a speechwriter and public relations staffer for the commission's executive director, General Charles Boyd (USAF ret). Authoring commission reports constitutes a form of political writing like no other. The process, as we will see in Chapter 10, practically invites writers to break every rule of good writing they have ever learned; but it is an invitation that can and should be refused.

After the Hart-Rudman Commission's work was done, I returned to *The National Interest* as editor. Now my apprenticeship was over; instead of being staff, I had and directed staff. After a few years, right around the time I was getting the hang of my post as editor, I left the magazine in the heady months following the terrorist attacks of September 11, 2001, to work for the then Secretary of State Colin L. Powell. I became a member of the Policy Planning staff of the U.S. State Department (S/P, which stands for Secretary/Policy), working in the main as one of Secretary Powell's three speechwriters.

As a State Department writer, I helped Secretary Powell prepare several major addresses and wrote essays (some based on speeches and some not), articles, and letters for his signature. A few of the articles were meant for publication in translation, which allowed me to learn a new skill through working with expert translators. In the diplomacy business, one can't be too careful with language—any language. It helped me that I had studied other languages, coming at least halfway close to mastering one or two.

Let me note at this point that it is indeed possible to become an excellent writer of English without knowing any other language. However, it is immensely more difficult, just as balancing oneself or anything else on one point is immensely more difficult than balancing on two or three. If you are reading this book knowing English as your second or third language, you may think yourself at a disadvantage compared to native English speakers. On the contrary. Actually, you have a richer perspective on what communications skills really entail, and that can prove to be a tremendous asset as you grow professionally and as a writer.

After Secretary Powell left office, I continued for a few months in 2005 as an S/P staffer and speechwriter for his successor, Dr. Condoleezza Rice. I helped Secretary Rice with her first two major addresses as Secretary of State—one in Paris and one in Tokyo. In that capacity, I traveled with her on Air Force II to more than two dozen countries and saw firsthand how she conducted impromptu in-flight press conferences. As different as they are in temperament and organizational styles, both Dr. Rice and General Powell taught me deeply valuable lessons about effective communication. I also was fortunate to be able to learn from the dozens of other government officials I came to know at the State Department, the Defense Department, and the White House.

After leaving the State Department, I became founding editor of *The American Interest* magazine. Thanks to the generosity and creative spirit of its publisher, Mr. Charles Davidson, and the support, friendship, and guidance of the magazine's editorial board chair, Dr. Francis Fukuyama, *The American Interest* has established itself as a must-read periodical for discerning minds the world over on issues of foreign policy, U.S. politics, and American culture. In Chapter 12, I will attempt to pass on to you some of the hard-won achievements I've earned as an editor.

Since I am about to teach you some tricks of the political writing trade, I tell you all this for a simple and straightforward reason: My experience of writing and publishing books, essays, and op-eds; of writing commission reports and speeches under the names of others;

and of composing more memos, award and ambassadorial swear-in ceremonials, memorial eulogies, and thank-yous than I frankly care to recall, means that I literally know what I am talking, or rather writing, about. Expertise is discounted these days as advertising language and culture has suffused our society. You deserve to know if those who presume to talk the talk have actually themselves walked the walk.

That may sound impressive, but there is one more thing you should know at this point. As Abraham Joshua Heschel once said, "It is easy to find people who will teach us how to be eloquent; but who will teach us how to be still?"[2] In other words, who will teach us how to listen, think, and reflect? Who will teach us the importance of quiet embarrassment as a source of curiosity, gratitude, compassion, and awe at the wonder of the world? Who will teach us how to appreciate our unearned life within the world? Politics and political persuasion are not the most important things any young person needs to learn in these days of 24/7 "wiredness" (more on neologisms follow). This is not a marginal or off-point observation. Writers are first human beings, and they cannot deploy their skills for good purposes without first understanding what it means to be a good human being.

If you have been following this narrative closely, you will likely understand something at once encouraging and sobering: Anyone can and most everyone who tries will learn to be a better writer; as I have just said, there is plenty of useful advice to help you become more eloquent and persuasive. But becoming a genuinely masterful writer is, for almost everyone, an arduous, protracted, and frustrating mountain climb. To reach your potential as a writer, whether of political tracts or anything else, you will need mentoring, support, and lots of practice. The way to learn what good writing is, simply enough, is to read a lot of good writing; the way to learn how to write well yourself is, also simply enough, to keep at it until you get there. Practice does not always or even usually make perfect—that's a lie, rather like the two-heads-are-better-than-one aphorism parsed earlier. But practice most certainly does make better.

So whatever merit you may find in this little book, and however helpful it may be to you, it is no substitute for your own disciplined effort.

---

2. Susannah Heschel, ed., *Abraham Joshua Heschel: Essential Writings* (Maryknoll, NY: Orbis Books, 2011), p. 158.

Cognitive psychologists tell us that it takes something like 10,000 hours to become a true expert in any task, whether it is learning to play the violin, becoming a cutting-edge medical researcher, or achieving fluency in, say, Bengali. The same goes for writing. Ultimately, there are no dramatic shortcuts. Yes, some people have more of an aptitude for writing than others, just as some people are better at carrying a tune and staying in rhythm than others (and there is a relationship between writing and music—we'll discuss that later). In the end, however, raw talent less-than-diligently developed will lose out to those willing to work long and hard to achieve their heart's desire. If you are truly determined to become an excellent writer, and an excellent persuasive writer in the world of politics, you will succeed roughly in proportion to the strength of that determination.

You probably have heard the axiom that "the pen is mightier than the sword" (although you may not know that the phrase was coined by the English author Edward Bulwer-Lytton in 1839 for his play *Richelieu: Or the Conspiracy*). I contend that Bulwer-Lytton's statement is untrue. If you are caught in a dark alley with someone who has it in for you, and he has a sword and you only a pen, you are in deep trouble. My advice would be to forget the pen and start moving as fast as you can in an otherly direction. But yes, the pen, or the keyboard, often is more *influential* than the sword, or the AK-47. (Word choices really do matter—that's the point here.)

So you are onto something genuinely important. Start your quest by taking a deep breath, because you will need all the oxygen you can get on your long journey up and over the mountain.

POLITICAL WRITING

1 FUNDAMENTALS OF RHETORIC AND POLEMIC

Before delving into the practical how-to tips on effective political writing, a little background is necessary. There is nothing whatsoever about how to do anything in this first chapter, but there is a good deal about what it is you are actually doing when you write to persuade. Understanding the history and nature of the activity one is pursuing is ultimately critical to pursuing it effectively. It is as Terrence Deacon says: "Knowing how something originated often is the best clue to how it works."[1]

Take medical research as an example of the point. There is a lot to be said for enlightened tinkering in medical technology and for trial-and-error intuitive research into diagnostics and treatment. Much useful medical knowledge has been amassed that way over a long period in human history. But knowing something about chemistry and biology at their scientific foundations has served as a mighty accelerant to applied medical research in recent centuries, particularly so in recent decades, as we have learned to plumb the genetic code that constitutes the operating system, so to speak, of our species. The same goes for political writing. Knowing the essential nature of the activity—how it was conceived and has grown over time—proves ultimately to be a key to effective praxis. So in this first chapter, we will learn about how political persuasion has been understood and taught in different times and places, and we will peer briefly into the foundational psycholinguistic nature of human persuasion in political life itself.

If you were to look up the word *rhetoric* in the dictionary, it would tell you more or less the following: Rhetoric is the art of using language to persuade or influence others. It would tell you, too, that the

---

1. Terrence W. Deacon, *The Symbolic Species: The Co-evolution of Language and the Brain* (New York: W.W. Norton, 1997), p. 23.

etymology of the word started in Greek and traveled through Latin to get to us. If you were to look up the word *polemic*, you would find, perhaps to your surprise, that its root is from the Greek word for war. A polemic, originally a theological term, is defined as language used to create controversy in contesting a thesis or point of view.[2] Polemics is making war, or rather pursuing conflict, with words instead of literal, physical weapons. So rhetoric and polemic are closely related concepts, but they are not exactly the same.

To study rhetoric and the character of successful polemic is a very old pursuit. Indeed, if you were among the tiny fraction of elite men in Europe who received a formal education between the collapse of the Roman Empire and the advent of what we very loosely refer to as modernity in the sixteenth and seventeenth centuries, rhetoric would have been a major part of your curriculum, as would the grammar of Latin and Greek (the languages of the few historical classics available at that time), Christian theology, some mathematics, and maybe a smattering of law. By the High Middle Ages (that's the eleventh through the thirteenth centuries), rhetoric was one of only seven standard liberal arts subjects for those privileged enough to go to school; it was coupled with logic and grammar in what was known as the foundational *trivium* of all education.[3] The basic idea was that logic is the art of thinking;

---

2. Speaking of a dictionary, you need to get one if you aspire to be a truly effective writer. The kinds of dictionaries that come preloaded on your computer are generally not adequate. Words are like the atoms that make up molecules; they are the building blocks of sentences, which, when put together in paragraphs and larger agglomerations of meaning, end up as writing. So you need to grasp what words mean not just in a superficial sense, but in a deeper sense; otherwise, your sentences and paragraphs and all the rest can never be excellent. Etymology is mandatory because a dictionary is to writing what underwear is to a wardrobe: It's not something you usually want to draw attention to, but you still need it. I suggest having close to hand the *Oxford Dictionary of the English Language*, one of the most magnificent creations in the history of the English tongue. But any Webster's or *American Heritage* will do in a pinch.

3. Yes, the word *trivial* does derive from *trivium* (this question popped into your mind, yes?), but understanding the connection requires a bit of research. You could look it up (and you'd be well served to get into the habit), but in this case I'll save you part of the trouble: The trivium developed out of the *quadrivium*, and since three is less than four, the trivium became associated with something that was less than something else. Several centuries later, the more modern notion of the trivial emerged, long since detached from its origin. These things happen, albeit gradually, all the time.

grammar the art of forming symbols and combining them to express thought; and rhetoric the art of communicating thought from one mind to another—the adaptation of language to circumstance, in other words. Thus, rhetoric was understood by teachers and students alike to constitute a most practical pursuit as the terminus of prior understanding. (That's why I asked my students to read Aristotle's "Rhetoric and Poetics.")

Now, why was this? Why was rhetoric so important in premodern times? There are two classes of answers to this question. One, well grasped by our forebears, is rather pedestrian, though still important to understand; the other is surprisingly philosophical in nature. Let us take these briefly in turn.

What were formally educated individuals (almost exclusively males) doing in those premodern days? What were they seeking through their learning in the first place? In the main, they were preparing for the sorts of careers befitting their social station, positions that would have been situated particularly in cities where politics tended to happen (as it still does today in most places) in the thickest and most consequential ways. (Landed aristocrats, whose fortunes and status lay in agriculture, were in general less apt to concern themselves with educating their young men in language arts, but this varied widely from place to place and from time to time.) And what were those urban careers? One might seek work in law or politics. One might become a military officer. One might become a physician. One might become a clergyman, or, with a basis in the approved faith of the time, a scholar and an educator.

All of these professions put a premium on knowing how to be persuasive, whether to argue in court, to fight the battles of theology and persuade one's flock or one's students, to command troops, or to get and bend the ear of the prince and the royal court. Indeed, the Greek idea of the *agora*, the public square, is the original direct democracy of the city-states, where the purest form of political rhetoric ever existed. Language was deemed important because it was clearly of enormous practical use to those who mastered it.

Note that for the most part, these examples refer to oral language, and this for the simple reason that before Johannes Gutenberg, and for several centuries after his invention of moveable type around 1450, most Europeans could neither read nor write. Therefore, the educated needed to speak to people, not write to them. The same was true generally outside the Western world. What was written was mostly "scholastic" in nature, which means that in Europe and its eventual colonial append-ages it remained largely within the Church—the Catholic Church, for that was the only religious establishment within the broader culture until well into the sixteenth century.

What was written was not, however, simply theological in character. On the contrary, all elements of human knowledge fell into the ambit of the scholastic tradition; it is just that the master narrative was a re-ligious one, and so all study and writing and rhetoric had to conform at least loosely to the premises of faith. The tradition of skilled polemic, in writing more than in speaking, arose within the scholastic tradi-tion, and while it certainly encompassed theology, it engaged issues of formidable range and complexity. Not least among them was how the clergy should be organized and how the Church should and should not relate to temporal authority. And so the premodern polemical traditions of religion-dominated discourse adapted themselves readily to Nicolaus Copernicus's sun-centered universe. The Church "fathers" were deep into politics all along. Nowhere is the bridge from the old to the new clearer than in the way the English author Thomas Hobbes wrote *Leviathan* (1651), one of the three or four most influential books of all time on political philosophy.

The tradition of teaching students how to form arguments, how to articulate them in speech, and how to write them down is as old as it is controversial. You can see in Socrates's opposition to writing itself—a testimony we have only because his student Plato wrote it down—a foundational controversy about the nature of human virtue as regards language.[4] You can see controversy, too, in Aristotle's view of the tension between emotion and reason in the design and deliv-ery of rhetorical discourse. Aristotle was bothered by the flamboyant trickery of the courts. Like Benjamin Franklin in a different time and place, he loathed lawyers. He urged educators to stress logic as well as the dramatic arts when they taught young people how to think and act, how to speak and listen, and how to read and write. He refused to countenance an understanding or teaching of rhetoric that reduced it to a guide to unscrupulous manipulation.

---

4. See *Phaedrus,* a dialogue between Socrates and Phaedrus, written around 370 B.C.E.

Socrates never stood a chance in his arguments against writing, although his opinions were, and in the philosophical tense remain, quite powerful. The schism between emphasizing logic versus style never really went away in education. Especially during the Enlightenment, also known as the Age of Reason (ca. 1660–1789 C.E.), educators in rhetoric differed vociferously on whether to stress logic and content or emotion and style. The pre-Enlightenment inclination of the Middle Ages (ca. 500–1500 C.E.) toward stressing style over logic carried over almost unmolested into the Enlightenment itself, proving, if nothing else, how conservative and ponderous educational institutions can be. But eventually, as the Age of Reason gained traction in European culture, the pendulum began to swing back toward Aristotle's predilection, thanks in part to the remarkable seventeenth-century political thinker John Locke. The underlying reason for this, most likely, is that as the rigid "estates" of the feudal era began to give way to the rumblings of early modern capitalism, education in rhetoric acquired another purpose: the general refinement of manners, taste, and social sensibility as the number and social diversity of educated people expanded. One learned to speak well in order to climb the social ladder, or to move sideways to benefit within one's own social class. Rhetoric merged to a considerable extent with the generic category of manners, which has a fascinating and hardly trivial social history of its own.[5]

Eventually, an even more expansive form of Enlightenment ideals held that when individuals refined their minds, all of society benefitted. This idea still holds true today: It is the bedrock justification, ultimately, for a liberal arts education. That is good to know, because the gargantuan costs of such an education, at least in the United States, can no longer be predicated on the strict economic recompense graduates can expect to gain from it.

Note, too, that the study of language and rhetoric through the ages inevitably collided with larger intellectual and social realities. So, for example, when educated classes in early modern times (ca. 1600) began to separate learning in general from theological frameworks, Latin and Greek were pushed to the side to make way for the emergence of colloquial languages—English, French, Italian, Dutch, and so forth. It was only in the seventeenth century that most of these languages finally

---

5. See Mark Caldwell, *A Short History of Rudeness: Manners, Morals, and Misbehavior in Modern America* (New York: Picador, 1999).

acquired systematic written forms; before that, again in the West at least, only classical languages were committed much to paper—Latin, Greek, and, very occasionally by European non-Jews, Hebrew.

Just a century or so later, the colloquial languages had become dominant. Why? The proliferation of printing presses certainly helped, but the phenomenon was also tied to the development of nationalism in the first modern nation-states. The raising up and formalization of colloquial language is a process we see in every European society and in every maturing European state in the seventeenth through the nineteenth and twentieth centuries. Some languages are relatively new in formalized written form: Estonian, Finnish, Hungarian, and Gaelic are some noteworthy examples.

As the English, Scots, Dutch, Danes, Swedes, French, and other Europeans developed a sense of themselves as separate nations, they nonetheless remained affected by pan-European ideas of the past. Some of the major influences, like the Holy Roman Empire, were religious in character, but others were broader than that. Starting from the Italian Renaissance and marching across Europe in the 1600s and 1700s, for example, a trend toward the neoclassical arose in Europe, embracing the forms of ancient Greece and Rome. Frederick the Great of Prussia built Sanssouci in Potsdam, with a spanking new Greco-Roman ruin he could see out his back door. (It's still there, by the way.) In architecture, literature, and, yes, rhetoric, the Europeans of that day held up Athens and Rome as models for emulation. They read Aristotle, but also Cicero, Seneca, and Cato. And as they did, they reinforced the understanding of rhetoric as a subject of key importance, a veritable portal to professional success and social refinement.

This was so on the Continent, but also in England, and from England neoclassicism came to America. Look at the libraries of Thomas Jefferson and James Madison to see whom the Founders read and tried to emulate. They studied the Greeks and Romans, too. But their language metaphors also came from a literary canon that included the Bible and related Christian religious works, especially Protestant ones. Mainly from these two sources, in ways they themselves could not have understood, John Locke and Charles de Montesquieu, Thomas Hobbes and Jean-Jacques Rousseau, Baruch Spinoza and Immanuel Kant, Alexis de Tocqueville and John Stuart Mill created modern political thought out of the classical and the biblical. They took the forms from the classical age, and the moral content from the Bible and its Enlightenment-era expositors, and blended them together against the backdrop of the new scientific Age of Reason. When they did, rhetoric gradually lost its pride of place among educators. New subjects ranging from Newtonian physics and related mathematical concepts to engineering soon emerged and could be formally taught. There was more to know, and so there was less time to focus on how one spoke within the schemes of formal education.

The understanding and uses of rhetoric also changed for social reasons. The wealthier classes grew with the advent of modern capitalism. The rise of the middle class brought with it increased economic specialization, urbanization, and literacy. More people wished to—and did—educate their children, mainly their sons, at first. So educators had to broaden their offerings and adjust their techniques. The many books we have in the Western tradition about education as both philosophy and vocation—like Rousseau's *Émile*, to take the best-known example—and the formal "science" of education itself, date from that time.

The arch conservatism of the universities, including their wish to teach rhetoric in the old ways, remained a strong current for a long time. Even into the 1820s in the United States some universities continued to hold their commencement and baccalaureate ceremonies in Latin. That is why undergraduate diplomas from Ivy League schools, as well as many others, are still written in Latin. But the old way of teaching rhetoric diverged ever more sharply from the sensibilities of the new classes. Students began to object, just as tenth graders in recent times have resented being forced to read *Beowulf*, Shakespeare's sonnets, and other (to them) indecipherable and apparently pointless tracts.

If anything, European universities were vastly more conservative than American ones. In France before 1789, those who saw rhetoric as central to education and emphasized its dramatic, nonrational, or arational elements appealed to a class in decline: a rather foppish bunch of aristocratic patriarchs who wore womanly clothing, silly wigs, refused to pay taxes, purchased instead of earned state and ecclesiastical offices, and delighted in figuring out ways to steal land from its less-well-positioned owners. Seeing rhetoric this way was of a piece with the whole aura of the ancien régime, and when that regime fell, first in France and then all across Europe aided by the armies of Napoleon Bonaparte, so in due course did the old concepts of teaching rhetoric.

In the New World, especially its English-speaking parts, the retreat of rhetoric as a formal part of the curriculum proceeded even faster and more thoroughly in a more egalitarian-minded, less class-stratified and class-conscious society. Teaching writing remained part of English language instruction, of course, at basic levels before university. Memorizing classical literature, especially poetry, was something every nineteenth-century student had to do, and "diction" was taught for the benefit of class presentations.[6] But at the university level, the formal teaching of rhetoric all but disappeared, particularly in the large number of new American colleges and universities founded after the Jacksonian era (roughly the second quarter of the nineteenth century).

Thus far we have said little about the non-Western history of rhetoric and polemic. One reason for this is that we are concerned here with the tradition of English-language rhetoric; another is that less is known about its non-Western origins. Suffice it to say that in premodern times, rhetoric formed a part of nearly every civilization's conception of education, whether in China and Japan, India and Persia, or beyond. All these cultures stressed oral as opposed to written arts, the most extreme example being that of Hindu culture. The only notable exception, for singular historical reasons, concerns the Jews, who stressed written over oral communication, and texts over speeches, with ramifications still discernable today. But the Mandarin system in China was also text oriented, and Muslim culture, too, focused heavily on the written word. This is largely because, among Muslims, language in all forms was art whenever it was not holy writ. Anti-iconographic in doctrine, Islamic arts focus heavily on words, including prose and poetry as well as calligraphy. The Persians in particular developed a keen sense of personal refinement, which included manners of persuasive speech. If, for example, you look to *Qabus-name*, Amir Nasir Unsur al-Ma'ani Kaikaus's eleventh-century book written for his son, Gilan Shah, you will discover a wonderful example of hardheaded yet elegant advice about the arts of political management and persuasion.

Why belabor all this in what is, in the main, a how-to book? To stress that the way language is conceived, taught, appreciated, and used is a function of culture. You will be writing your way into an English-speaking culture in early twenty-first-century America that regards *rhetoric* as a mildly dirty word. The connotation of the word these days equates either to the use of language as a frill or to a not

---

6. You can get a sense of what students learned, and the methods teachers used to impart it, by studying the series of *McGuffey's Readers* that became ubiquitous in American classrooms after the Civil War, and which remained popular in many places into the 1920s.

well-hidden suspicion that someone is trying to pull the wool over your eyes. "Oh, that's just a bunch of rhetoric," you hear people say, meaning that what is being put forth is off point, excessive, irrelevant, or designed to mislead. The word also carries a musty, antique odor, rather like the words *virtue, sin,* and, increasingly, *truth.* But, then again, the United States is also the only place on the planet where the phrase "that's history" is employed to mean "that's irrelevant," passé, of no practical interest whatsoever. Aristotle would be appalled, but what can one expect rhetoric's cultural cachet to be in contemporary America if history doesn't even rate a respectable hearing?

None of this means that Americans no longer care about language. The academy certainly cares about it, as the terms *philology, semiotics, semantics,* and *linguistics* imply. All these subjects are taught and written about at our universities; the literature on each fills whole libraries for large numbers of graduate students to explore. Modern Western philosophy, too, is unusually concerned with language, and the intelligentsia more generally is deeply interested in the ways and means of communications within our society's cultural and technological context. From Ludwig Wittgenstein to Marshall McLuhan, the twentieth century in the West was virtually obsessed with the problematics of language and meaning. Now, in the twenty-first century, this obsession has been coupled to rapidly advancing brain science research that is unlocking insight after insight about the neurophysiological underpinnings of the symbolic construction process that is the sine qua non of human language.

All that notwithstanding, only a very few schools (among them, the University of California at Berkeley and Texas A&M University) teach rhetoric at any level of formal education. My undergraduate UCDC course in political writing was, to the best of my knowledge, the only one of its kind in the country at the time. I searched high and low for syllabi to help me prepare the course and failed to find a single one. I found courses on writing, usually in English departments—some devoted to fiction writing, some designed to help nonnative English speakers, some more broadly remedial in character. There is even an offering in The Great Courses, a for-profit lectures-on-DVD program that runs out of Chantilly, Virginia, on "Building Great Sentences: Exploring the Writer's Craft," delivered by Brooks Landon of the University of Iowa. The lecture series consists of 24 titles on topics such as "The Rhythm of Cumulative Syntax," "Degrees of Suspensiveness," and "Prefab Patterns for Suspense." I listened to a fair bit of this, and there is plenty of good advice here once you make your way through the academic jargon. But this has nothing to do with rhetoric as Aristotle, Locke, or Madison would have understood it. A recent search has turned up only a few for-credit courses on political writing.[7]

What this means for all practical purposes is that if you want to master a subject that the premoderns considered to be unarguably mandatory to a serious and practical education, you cannot readily do it in school. It means you have to do it the old-fashioned way—by apprenticeship to a magazine editor, a professional speechwriter, or an advertising executive. In a sense, the situation with regard to rhetoric, polemic, and the arts of political persuasion in general is a little like law school's relation to what goes on in courtrooms. Some younger folk imagine that going to law school will teach them how to comport themselves in a courtroom. It does no such thing. To learn how to be a successful lawyer you have to apprentice yourself to a law firm and raise your skills through example and experience. If you are ruthlessly exploited in the process by those above you in this professional version of a Ponzi scheme, that's the way it goes. Don't say no one warned you.

You know the old saying that every dark storm cloud has a silver lining? This is yet another one of those comforting lies we tell each other. Dark storm clouds often drop hail on you, fix to drown you, or try to skewer you with lightning. That said, in this case there is a scintilla of truth to the aphorism. Skill with language, written and oral, is as important today as it was in Aristotle's time. It's just that most people are at best only vaguely aware of this, and the vast majority is much too lazy to do anything about it. So you have a significant relative advantage in recognizing where leverage lies, and your relative advantage will grow as your skills mature. That's your silver lining from what is, in general, a depressing circumstance.

You may think that we could at this point skip to the how-to stuff and get on with the show without missing anything important, but you would be mistaken. Just one more bit of intellectual preparation remains before we can launch into the how-to aspect of this book.

---

7. But there is no textbook, save for Giandomenico Majone, *Evidence, Argument & Persuasion in the Policy Process* (New Haven: Yale University Press, 1989). The book is maybe a bit stuffy and occasionally arcane, but the author is on the right track when it comes to the nature of political argumentation and persuasion.

You need to understand why and how language matters specifically in politics. Having made the simpler point that rhetoric is a function of culture, and that you had better be aware of the one in which you live and work, let us now briefly examine the more esoteric but also more interesting philosophical aspects of the topic.

We have noted in passing that from the very start, from Athens and Aristotle, differences of view arose about the relation of drama to logic in human speech and, by consequence, the arts of rhetoric, giving the teaching and practice of rhetoric a controversial edge. The controversy came down to the way different schools of thought explained the origins and character of human consciousness. They wondered where their inner selves—the voice in each respective head—came from, and they began to ask questions about the relationship between the empirical, physical qualities of human beings and these immaterial, rather elusive aspects. In other words, they turned the question of human thinking into an object of thinking. That is the most basic definition of what philosophy is all about. As you also probably know, the Greeks never reached consensus on this question; they agreed to disagree, which is why we still have philosophy departments in universities today.

They did agree on certain premises, however. One was that the human capacity for articulate speech sets our species apart from all others. Naturally, then, some of the ancients likely asked themselves, what's the relationship between the tools we use to think, namely words, and *what* we think? Thus was born one of the five branches of philosophy: epistemology, namely, the study of how we know what we know. The other four branches—logic, ethics,[8] cosmology, and aesthetics—also depend to one degree or another on understanding the relationship between the human capacity for symbolization (but not just through the use of words) and the subjects of interest to which symbolization is applied.

The ancient Greeks also understood—and eighteenth-century Enlightenment philosophers emphasized—that in all human endeavors, language-based thought merges our rational capacities with our "passions," or what we today call our emotions or affective side. Our cognitive virtues are driven into action by our purposes, by what we

---

8. Contrary to increasingly common usage, ethics is not a synonym for morality. Morality refers to behavior. Ethics is the *study* of morality. You will often find locutions in which the speaker or writer mentions both together, usually separated by the word "and." This means that the speaker does not actually know the meaning of these words. Don't be that person.

want and do not want for ourselves and others about whom we care. Our rational capacities in consciousness are thus driven and directed by emotions that accounts for the bulk of what our brains are actually doing at any given waking moment. As William James (1842–1910) recognized more than a century ago, and as brain research corroborates today, "Our normal waking consciousness, rational consciousness as we call it, is but one special type of consciousness, whilst all about it, parted from it by the filmiest of screens, there lie potential forms of consciousness entirely different."[9]

If our rational capacities cohabit with a vast range of preconscious neural activity, it follows that our emotions permeate all human thought and speech (and writing). We cannot readily think without language, and we cannot speak or write without thinking—although I have to admit that here in Washington this latter proposition sometimes begs special proof. It is not true that articulate speech is a precondition for all thought, or else chimps and gray parrots and whales would not be what they are. But it does seem to be a precondition for the kind of symbolic cognitive operations that allow humans to conceive a concrete past and project a concrete future. We are capable of abstraction, which allows us to extract models of behavior from experience, our own and observations of others, and reinsert those models anywhere we like for fun, profit, and, occasionally, understanding.

What this means, in short, is that humans are a promiscuously associational species. When we are not bringing to bear our rational critical facilities on some problem, we are swept into a kind of omnidirectional free association in which our passions point the way. We all recognize this state of mind from dreams. But even when we are wide awake we are still dreaming, albeit below the level of conscious, directed activity. Every seemingly rational twenty-first-century human walks around with a totemistic, mythological soul nestled deeply within, and we do this in social concert because we are undeniably social animals. Our less cultivated, primitive, and generally cautious, if not anxious, self is never very far from bursting into consciousness, and on reflection we all know what tends to bring out this more primal self: fear. We are all born capable of experiencing fear of enemies, fear of the unknown, fear of being alone, fear of meaninglessness, and, above all, fear of death in the foreknowledge of our mortality.

---

9. William James, *The Varieties of Religious Experience* (1902).

In other words, both our individual and communal senses of reality are vulnerable to disruption. When we get emotional, in particular, our modes of thought and speech better reflect the analogic and even mimetic thinking of earlier, mythic epochs of humankind than they do the scientific-rational thinking we suppose is our norm. In a sense, when we become emotional we tend to revert. Let one fairly well-known example illustrate the point.

In December 1941, Admiral Husband E. Kimmel was commander of the U.S. fleet at Pearl Harbor. After the Japanese attack of December 7, Admiral Kimmel tried to reverse engineer the misperception that led him and his junior officers to be surprised by what had just happened. In calm retrospect, he and others realized that they actually had in hand all of the information they needed to anticipate the Japanese attack, but they had framed the pieces of information within a set of expectations that prevented them from seeing the pieces in the right way. But Admiral Kimmel's famous first reaction was not that the attack *did* not happen, but that it *could* not happen. He saw before his eyes the flames and destruction, but he still insisted that what was happening could not be happening. He was not crazy in any conventional sense; rather, he was momentarily disoriented by acute emotional ataxia—in this case by assaults of guilt and fear. In a way, his state of mind briefly flirted with a mode of magical thinking characteristic of humankind during hunter-gatherer times, or of those in the grasp of certain hallucinogenic drugs.

Sometimes entire societies are gripped by such levels of fear and uncertainty that they seem, from the perspective of others at least, to go crazy. The reason, simply put, is that politics is made up of two parts: "how" questions and "why" questions. "How" questions can be approached dispassionately and analytically, at least in theory. We need to refurbish our infrastructure; fine. What's the most cost-effective way to do that? Again, in theory at least, we can gather together a group of engineers, urban development experts, and financiers and work out a plan. No one would necessarily need to get hot under the collar, lose their temper, raise their voice, or stomp out of the room (even though these things frequently happen anyway). "Why" questions, however, are a different story.

"Why" (and sometimes "what") questions in politics churn emotions by definition. Why are we organized as we are in this society today, as opposed to how we used to be organized or how other societies are organized? Why are some people richer and more powerful than others?

What is fair? Is our system of justice adequately impartial? What role does the state play in my private life, and where are the correct boundaries between public and private spheres? Within societies and perhaps especially between and among different societies, argument over such questions can become very intense and even lead to violence. All societies develop templates to explain and manage these kinds of questions. Taken together, they form a political cosmology, or what we commonly call an *ideology.*

Sometimes people think they are self-aware of their ideology, and political leadership sometimes talks in openly ideological fashion, as in twentieth-century fascism and communism. In these two cases, and especially in the latter, the claim was that the ideology was objectively correct, that it was scientific in nature. Needless to say, this wasn't true. But sometimes, most times in fact, ideological assumptions, which are always present in some form, just flow smoothly into everyday public life, disappearing into the flux of assumptions held more or less in common. That is how it has almost always been in the United States.

Other times, however, even this subterranean, assumed kind of ideology becomes explicit. It usually does so, ironically enough, when it becomes problematic—when it begins to fail to explain the reality for which it has arisen. As already suggested, it tends to become explicit when people are afraid, anxious, or unsettled. And it is inherent in the nature of ideological language that it is metaphorical/mythical in nature, not scientific/rational. Instead of separating out the parts of a causal matrix and looking upon them with an attitude of dispassion, as does science, metaphorical/mythical language pushes everything together in an atmosphere of emotional arousal. The anthropologist Clifford Geertz expressed this as follows:

> Science names the structure of situations in such a way that the attitude contained toward them is one of disinterestedness. Its style is restrained, sparse, resolutely analytic. . . . But ideology names the structure of situations in such a way that the attitude contained toward them is one of commitment. Its style is ornate, vivid, and deliberately suggestive: By objectifying moral sentiment through the same devices that science shuns, it seeks to motivate action.[10]

---

10. Clifford Geertz, "Ideology as a Cultural System," in David Apter, ed., *Ideology and Discontent* (New York: Free Press, 1964), p. 58.

The Princeton political philosopher Michael Walzer added that the very essence of the political symbol is that it simultaneously provokes thought and evokes feeling. "Words alone may not do this," he wrote, "but words which have become part of the special vocabulary of politics—king, subject, citizen, duty, rights, father of his country, checks and balances, and so on—obviously do."[11] Evocative symbols are part and parcel of modern nationalism, and when those symbols are words as opposed to images of the flag, say, they become *condensation symbols*. A condensation symbol has a strong emotional valence. From just one word or one phrase, a whole suitcase of emotional baggage may be thrown into public discourse—think of "Munich," "Sputnik," or "9/11."

Politics thus operates at a fairly abstract level, for what is the nation in any event but an abstraction? Indeed, the nature of the mythic mind expresses itself in politics whenever "why" questions are under discussion. Walzer continued:

> Politics is an art of unification; from many, it makes one. And symbolic activity is perhaps our most important means of bringing things together, both intellectually and emotionally. . . . In a sense, the union of men can only be symbolized; it has no palpable shape or substance. The state is invisible; it must be personified before it can be seen, symbolized before it can be loved, imagined before it can be conceived.[12]

With this observation we are brought toward the end of this brief lesson. Some kinds of language—written and oral—better reflect our rational side, while other kinds better reflect our emotional side. The kinds of political behavior, thought, and rhetoric that raise our pulse align with mythic consciousness far better than with the language of scientific rationality. There is a characteristic form of language that does this. Again, within ideological language, whether the ideology is recognized for what it is or hidden from conscious presumption, *the symbolic processes of metaphor are at work*. The effectiveness of "oversimplified" metaphorical images derives not from the desire to deceive the uninformed or excite the unreflective, but, wrote Geertz,

---

11. Michael Walzer, "On the Role of Symbolism in Political Thought," *Political Science Quarterly*, 82: 2 (June 1967), p. 195n.

12. *Ibid.*, p. 194.

from its capacity to grasp, formulate, and communicate social realities that elude the tempered language of science. . . . It may mediate more complex meanings than its literal reading suggests. . . . [I]t appears to be a metaphor.[13]

When people are afraid, the sway of mythic consciousness grows. And since people are always at least a little existentially anxious, some mythical thinking is always afoot. We know this even from brain scans. When people are worried, when they argue, when their honor is impugned, when their pocketbooks are attacked, when they are confused by events, mythic consciousness and modes of reasoning fire up from the older parts of our brain.

But we know this even more vividly from history. The philosopher Ernst Cassirer witnessed the rise of Nazism, a deeply arational, violent, and murderous movement. He saw mythic consciousness spring into the center of the political arena in one of the most intellectually sophisticated countries in Europe. This led him to conclude that

in politics we are always living on volcanic soil. . . . For myth has not really been vanquished and subjugated. . . . Even in primitive societies where myth prevails and governs the whole of man's social feeling and social life it is not always operative in the same way nor does it always appear with the same strength. It reaches its full force when man has to face an unusual and dangerous situation.[14]

Now let us make the obvious connection that will get us to the how-to part of this book. When we write about politics, which subjects do we choose? Subjects where we all agree already? Subjects where nothing of real importance is at stake? Of course not. Political language is unvaryingly about problematics, and hence it is inherently emotional at some level. It is therefore inherently open to the infiltration of modes of mythic consciousness and thought, and to manipulation by dint of language suffused with metaphor.

Think about it for just a few seconds, and you will see the point. What do effective political speeches do? Do they analyze and separate and make distinctions, or do they merge and conflate? Do they teach,

---

13. Geertz, "Ideology as a Cultural System," p. 66.
14. Ernst Cassirer, *The Myth of the State* (New Haven: Yale University Press, 1945), pp. 278–80.

or do they motivate? Do they inform, or do they reassure? Political language is not didactic. Effective political language does not deliberately teach anyone anything, especially for its own sake. One of the first laws of political speechwriting at high levels, as we will see in Chapter 7, is that one should "never commit a truth." This does not mean that one should lie; it simply means that one should not tell a truth unless there is some persuasive purpose for doing so.

Am I saying that the way we reason about politics and the way we speak and write about it actually produce different patterns of brain activity in both the speaker and the listener then those patterns produced when we discuss what to have for dinner, how we should design a garage, and so on? Yes, I am. Decision making under normal conditions takes place, or rather is concentrated, in one part of the brain; decision making under stress occurs in another. Stress, in this case, is a synonym for emotion. And serious political debate is always stressful, always emotional, always potentially volcanic. That is why, as David Green has written,

> Language is the most powerful of human weapons. Armed force may keep people in a state of unwilling subjugation for years, even for generations. Only through language, however, can human understanding itself be manipulated and people brought to cooperate in their own subjugation. . . . The history of language and history of politics are inseparable; indeed, the evolution of word meanings is a record of ongoing struggles over the use of language as a political weapon. . . . Once language is recognized as the most fundamental political weapon, philology emerges as not only the basic historical science but the basic political science as well.[15]

Political writing is inherently manipulative. It takes advantage of the power of metaphor, and truly skillful writers know this is so even as the targets of their prose generally do not. In some ways, political writing is an aggressive, combative craft, and it becomes a gamelike one when it engages other political writing of different views.

Many young idealists are attracted to the political arena because they want to serve truth. What they eventually find is that, as Winston Churchill, the British prime minister during World War II, put it dur-

---

15. David Green, *Shaping Political Consciousness: The Language of Politics in America from McKinley to Reagan* (Ithaca, NY: Cornell University Press, 1987), p. ix.

ing Tehran Conference of 1943, "truth is so precious [in politics] that it must be attended by a bodyguard of lies." I don't mean to say that political writers start out when they compose an essay or an opinion column with the conscious intention of lying. I simply mean that in complex debates, truth is so elusive that points of view triumph by dint of subtleties, elisions, misdirection, selective presentations of facts, innuendo, and the statistical "imagination," let's call it, or they don't triumph at all. Everyone thinks he is in the right, but since that person realizes that the other side is just as devoted to its vision of what is right and wrong, there is nothing to do for it except to buy more ink and think more manipulative thoughts. This is why Peggy Noonan, President Reagan's principal speechwriter for some years, referred to her craft as a "dark art." She was perfectly correct, and I affirm her view despite the fact that I wrote speeches for two Secretaries of State neither one of whom ever once knowingly stated a mistruth to the public.

So if you think that in politics the truth sets anyone free, and that all you have to do to succeed is to let the facts speak for themselves, then you are in for a rude awakening. It doesn't work that way. Possibly the clearest explanation of why this is so comes from none other than Niccolò Machiavelli, who has gotten a bad rap in recent centuries from churchy sorts of people. Summarizing very well what we today recognize as a collective action problem, he wrote in Chapter 15 of *The Prince:*

> He who neglects what is done for what ought to be done, sooner effects his ruin than his preservation; for a man who wishes to act entirely up to his professions of virtue soon meets with what destroys him among so much that is evil. Hence it is necessary for a prince wishing to hold his own to know how to do wrong, and to make use of it or not according to necessity.

It's sad, perhaps, but this is as true today as it was when Machiavelli found the courage to say it so long ago. If this bothers you, then perhaps a profession in or around politics is not for you after all.

Recommended Reading

"Rhetoric," in A.C. Kors, ed., *The Encyclopedia of the Enlightenment* (New York: Oxford University Press, 2003), vol. 4, pp. 458–61.

Lane Cooper, trans., *The Rhetoric of Aristotle* (New York: Prentice Hall, 1960).

W.D. Ross, *Aristotle* (1923; 6th ed., New York: Routledge, 2004), ch. 9, "Rhetoric and Poetics."

Ernst Cassirer, *An Essay on Man: An Introduction to a Philosophy of Human Culture* (New Haven, CT: Yale University Press, 1944).

Writing Exercise

Collect three English-language definitions of the term *rhetoric* from three different centuries, and then compare and contrast them in a maximum 500-word essay.

2   BECOMING A BETTER WRITER

Before getting down to the specifics of political persuasion, let's begin with some basic observations about writing well—even when the subject and purpose have little or nothing to do with politics. The first point, while of extreme importance, may surprise you: Writing and reading are not natural to human beings. Speaking and listening are natural, and in certain critical ways articulate speech defines our species. But there is a huge gap, both conceptually and historically, between speaking and listening on the one hand, and writing and reading on the other. You will note that many thousands of years elapsed between the advent of the human as speaker and the advent of the human as writer. The development of writing and reading, and the maturation of both from simple sign making and record keeping into true symbolic metaphorical expression is more or less synonymous with the advent and advance of civilization. If, as the American soprano Beverly Sills once said, "art is the signature of civilizations"—and it is—then writing is the necessary instrument that fills in the letter above the signature.[1]

The point of writing about anything for any purpose (with the single exception of diaries meant for only one's own eyes in some near or distant future) is to communicate something to others. That something does not have to be anything concrete or objective. For instance, sometimes a writer wants to communicate emotion; that's what poetry is principally about. But whatever it is that one wishes to communicate to others, it follows that the quality of what is written is closely related to the quality of what one wishes to communicate. Put

---

1. Some of you may not recognize the name Beverly Sills. She was a famous opera singer who died in 2007. Since we are speaking of civilization, you might as well understand now that to be part of a civilization you should be well versed in its essential biography as it accumulates over time. When you come upon a name in your reading that you do not recognize, you should make a note to find out who the person is or was. This discipline is similar to the one that will have you look up words you do not know, but on a different plane.

as simply as possible, and hopefully without offending anyone, this means that if you don't know how to think, you cannot learn how to write. It is not strictly true that you must have something worth saying before you can say it well; after all, plenty of people wax eloquent while saying quite stupid things. (After all, as I have already pointed out, I am writing this in Washington.) But it does help to write with a purpose: As in the *trivium* of old, logic and concept must precede effective communication.

At the risk of being politically incorrect, allow me to point out that some people are brighter than others, some more creative than others, and some more energetic intellectually than others. I am not speaking here about raw intelligence, or at least not about that alone. I am talking more about a person's orientation toward learning and knowledge—matters of character rather than intelligence. In most cases, it all comes down to whether someone respects knowledge and grasps the difficulties involved in attaining it. Someone who respects a given subject is, in the end, far more likely to be able to speak and write intelligently about it than someone who does not.

Even more sensitive a matter is the equally disturbing (to some) observation that some people are not as interesting or as interested in intellectual pursuits—which is to say, have any obvious intellectual curiosity—as others. A style of writing is ultimately a personal matter, even when it comes to rhetoric and polemic. A writer's style invariably reflects her personality, as well as her level of intellectual curiosity; the more textured the personality, the more sophisticated and appealing the writing. Since a person's character continues to develop and ripen with age and experience, it follows that one's writing style will not remain static. It tracks character all the way to the cemetery. It is a rare sentient being who writes as well at age 30 as he does at age 60, just because that 60 year old is a more experienced, more nuanced, and usually a far more interesting character than he was half a life before.

What this means, among other things, is that you need not beat yourself up for not getting the hang of excellent writing in a short time. It is quite possible to be hellaciously smart—downright prodigy material even—but still have trouble translating your gift into writing. Like making a great piecrust, writing is a touch skill. (The presumption buried in the common phrase "easy as pie" is another one of those great whoppers we tell each other all the time, by the way. Making a good piecrust is not easy at all.) It is good to know, therefore, as Robert Cormier, the American author of *The Chocolate War,* said: "The beautiful part of writing is that you don't have to get it right the first time, unlike, say, a brain surgeon."

All that said, even the less interested and curious among us can learn to write better if they try hard enough. The first step is to learn how to *think* better and, if you are a student of one kind or another, how to *study* better.

The best piece of advice anyone will ever give you about learning to study effectively is this: Put what you are learning into your own words. That means taking notes rather than recording lectures. It means taking notes rather than underlining or highlighting text in your books. Recording and underlining are passive ways of trying to learn. You may be able to recollect discrete facts from this method, but you will have a harder time integrating what you are learning: The material you are trying to learn is more likely to stick—to become part of you as a vessel of maturing knowledge—if you recast it into your own words.

Furthermore, by putting what you are trying to learn in your own words and sharing your knowledge by engaging other students, outside of class as well as within it, you accomplish two goals: reinforcing your own learning while communicating your insights with others. You may think that you are saving time by underlining or highlighting text in your books; actually, you are engaged in the most inefficient way of studying that exists. Without realizing it, you are actually wasting time, not saving it. (Don't even *think* about underlining or highlighting the previous sentences!)

A second excellent piece of advice is to keep track of how you use your time. There is no shortcut for most people when it comes to learning difficult material. It just takes time. All else being equal, the greater the number of hours you can spend thinking about a given subject, the more confidently you will learn it, not just in its broad strokes but in its nuances and details. How much time do you spend surfing through the internet in a given week? How much time do you spend on Facebook and other social networking sites? How much time do you spend watching television? These are colossal squanderings of your precious time—especially television, because it is the most passive in its essential nature. The concept of opportunity costs is relevant here. Every hour you spend watching television is not just an hour spent watching television; it is an hour not spent either studying or doing something intellectually useful, such as practicing a musical instrument or getting some exercise. The only way to get some control over how you use your time is by determining a reliable way to keep track of it. So start doing that immediately. I will leave the method to you.

As I have already mentioned, to appreciate good writing you have to appreciate good reading. In a very real sense, the bridge between your study habits and your capacity to express yourself is one of translation—having the ability to recognize quality in what you read and then reproduce that quality in what you write. It follows that to make such a translation, you need something to translate. This means you should read a lot, and you should be reading in a certain way.

Whatever your special interests, you have a choice as to whether to read very deeply into a narrow specialty or to read broadly across a range of related subjects. The wisest course for most people is to create a balance between depth and breadth. In social science, for example, people who are interested in politics should read not only political science and government materials but also the best works they can find in sociology and especially anthropology. All social scientists should also read history and philosophy. It is this balance between intensity and breadth that stands the best chance of giving you a genuine competitive edge in your field of choice.

In addition, you should be reading fiction of the highest quality. Of course, what qualifies as "high quality" is to some extent a matter of taste; yet, certain classics have withstood the test of time and have validated their quality across generations. If you need suggestions as to what fiction to read, all you have to do is asked professionals and mentors whom you trust, and I assure you that they will pour suggestions your way. Many will rush to lend you books as well.

There are two key reasons why you should always be reading fiction. First, writers of fiction invariably pay more attention to matters of style and grace then do writers of nonfiction, and so the best models for style and grace are to be found there, whether in novels, short stories, or poetry.

Second, there are certain truths about human nature that ramify through all the social sciences and are better expressed in fiction than in nonfiction. A novelist has a certain license to express himself in a manner, as Dean Acheson, President Harry S. Truman's Secretary of State once said, that is "clearer than truth,"[2] and there are certain un-

---

2. As quoted by James Chace in *Acheson: The Secretary of State Who Created the American World* (Cambridge, MA: Harvard University Press, 1999).

deniable advantages in being able to do that. Let's take, for example, the very popular concern about economic development and poverty eradication in what used to be called the Third World. The literature in this field is outrageously dismal, so much so that anyone who truly cares about the political dimensions of this very serious subject should read Joseph Conrad's novel *Nostromo*. Published in 1904, *Nostromo* is about a fictional Latin American country, but it gives away nothing in insight to contemporary problems with poverty and injustice the world over.

There is yet another reason for reading fiction: It relaxes you. A few pages read in the evening in bed before lights out can sweeten your dreams (unless, of course, you are reading Stephen King). This is not, as you may suppose, just a fringe benefit from reading fiction. Your creativity cannot blossom if you are always under stress. Genuine sophistication intellectually is a function of a dialectic between strict thinking and loose thinking, and to do your share of loose thinking you need to be relaxed.

It's also a good idea in this regard to vary the places where you study, read, and think. If all you do when you are working is stare at a screen or at objects in a room that are no farther than a few feet away from you, you are doing yourself a disservice. Get outside; find vistas to feed your imagination. Look into the distance from time to time and let your eyes adjust to it; this flexes your brain. There are no guarantees, but you might be amazed at what this little exercise can do for you.

That, too, is partly what fiction is for: It is a metaphorical way to change your perspective, to think at different relative distances. It is exactly as Sven Birkerts said in his 1994 book *The Gutenberg Elegies: The Fate of Reading in an Electronic Age*:

> I often find that a novel . . . can become a blur to me soon after I've finished it. I recollect perfectly the feeling of reading it, the mood I oc-cupied, but I am less sure about the narrative details. It is almost as if the book were, as [the Austrian-born philosopher and logician Ludwig] Wittgenstein said of his propositions, a ladder to be climbed and then discarded after it has served its purpose. . . . I read novels to indulge in a concentrated and directed inner activity that parallels—and thereby tunes up, accentuates—my own inner life.

You may think that with all your obligations to learn this and that you cannot afford to spend time reading fiction, but you would be wrong. You cannot afford *not* to spend some time reading fiction, especially not if you want to learn how to write well.

Earlier we described words as the atoms of language, and so it stands to reason that one of the tasks you must successfully complete in your quest to become a good writer is expanding your vocabulary. The more words you have mastered, the more distinctions you can make. To *select* is not the same as to *choose* and to *saunter* is not the same as to *amble* and I could go on and on. Knowing the differences allows you to fine-tune your expression. It allows you, as a seeker of persuasive skills, to target your prey with a stiletto instead of an elephant gun. Mark Twain, who once observed that there are no true synonyms in the English language, said it best: "The difference between the right word and the almost right word is the difference between lightening and the lightening bug."

More to the point of political writing, the words *country, nation, state,* and *nation-state* are most assuredly *not* synonyms. Each one means something distinct, yet Americans, in particular, for reasons we do not have time to examine, tend to use all four interchangeably, both in oral speech and in writing. Conflating all these terms leads to no end of confusion and misunderstanding. If you peruse a good dictionary, you will soon understand the differences. But to save you the trouble, I will give you the basics.

A country is a place, a land. It usually has borders in modern political life. A nation is a group of people who think they have enough in common to live together in a single political unit. Most nations are based on ethno-linguistic groups to one degree or another, but the degrees vary widely. A state is the political-administrative structure that rules the nation in the country. A nation-state is a normative term, dating from the nineteenth century, which either implicitly or otherwise asserts that a nation and a state should be coterminous—that, in other words, state sovereignty should be based on the national characteristics of the people. It is a term that was meant to disparage the idea of political legitimacy based on multiethnic empires. For better and for worse, it worked.

Some years ago, early in the fall semester, an enthusiastic 19-year-old student came up to me after class and told me that during the just elapsed summer he had "driven clear across the nation." I told him that he had just confessed to multiple vehicular homicide. His face took on the appearance of a dog that has just heard an ultrasonic noise, alert but deeply perplexed about its precise location. You will be relieved to learn that he eventually calmed down and got the point.

When you conflate terms like country, nation, state, and nation-state, what you are actually doing is disorganizing the accumulated stock of knowledge about political subjects for yourself and others. You are not only *not* saying or writing anything coherent when you misuse these terms, you are unraveling a coherence you have inherited but do not appreciate. Don't do this, please. Don't add to the problem, as the following example—an actual exam question for the fifth and sixth-grade levels from a monitoring tool used to predict scores on the Maryland state assessment (I could not possibly make this up, but a professional curriculum specialist did)—illustrates so vividly:

A nation is a _____.
A. building
B. city
C. country
D. statue

The correct answer, of course, is "none of the above," but that's not a choice.

There are clear ways to avoid such errors and to expand your vocabulary systematically. I have already mentioned two of them: Read broadly as well as in depth, and include fiction in your reading protocols. Obviously, if you read only narrowly in terms of subject matter, you will stunt your vocabulary growth. Instead, you must expose yourself to new words and to new uses of words as efficiently as possible.

I can guarantee you that this will never happen as a result of watching television, whose vocabulary is carefully dumbed down to a level that makes advertisers comfortable. And that is a very low level. To me, the epitome of what television does to vocabulary has been captured in electronic amber thanks to the 1980s animated show *The Smurfs*. In this insipid excuse for a cartoon, every time an opportunity arose for the show's writers to introduce even the slightest example of an interesting vocabulary word to children, the little blue people invariably employed the verb "to smurf." And they wondered back then why kids seemed always to be in a daze after a dose of *The Smurfs*.

But reading broadly is not enough. To build your vocabulary, you must be disciplined. Most people, when they encounter for the first time a word they do not know, skip over it or try to understand it from context. This is a mistake. When you see a word you do not know, or a word you sort of know but do not know well enough to use in your own writing, look it up in that dictionary I told you earlier to get your hands on; then, write down the meaning in your own words. It is not a bad idea to *keep a running list of new words* you have encountered and to review that list from time to time. Once you start using words from this list in your own speaking and writing, without exerting yourself specially to do so, it means that you have become comfortable with them, and you can remove them from the list as you add new words to it.

You do not have to interrupt your reading every time you encounter a new word in order to do this. One way of being disciplined about improving your vocabulary is to mark in light pencil in the margin of what you are reading with a number indicating which word in that line is the one you do not know. Then, after you have finished a section or chapter, you can go back and look up the words you have marked, and erase your pencil notations as you do. This is a very effective method not only for learning new words, but also for understanding what you have just read, for it is virtually certain that the words you don't know taken together form some kind of conceptual cluster. Once you master that cluster based on an investigation of these new words, you will have learned more than just vocabulary.

One way to measure your progress in vocabulary growth is to check your writing for vocabulary tedium. With the search function in word processing programs, this is easier to do than ever. If you sense, or if someone is good enough to tell you, that you are overusing certain words, you can count them in any given piece of writing on which you are at work. So do it. In particular, look for how many times you use variants of the verb "to be." Lazy writing defaults excessively to "is" and "was" and "are," so search for these words, thesaurus in hand, and ask yourself on a case-by-case basis if a better verb for your purposes may be substituted. Sometimes the verb "to be" is the right verb—see? So you don't have to get rid of them all. But if "lazy" unfortunately describes you as a writer, the fastest way to improve your compositional skills lies in a search-and-destroy mission aimed at the verb "to be."

Another way to conquer vocabulary poverty is to get into the habit of using a thesaurus. *Roget's* is the standard for English, and it is a wonderful resource for those who learn to consult it regularly. You should own one.

As important as vocabulary is to good writing, even more important is conceptual sophistication. You will again recall that the High Middle Ages *trivium* concerned logic and grammar before rhetoric. Not only must you be able to discern what ideas do and do not make sense, your obligation resides as well in being able to fashion symbolic delivery vehicles for your ideas before you wind up and fire off your personal rhetoric machine. One way to become more facile with conceptual language is to practice by using the insights of others. You can systematize this practice if you keep a quotation file.

As you read more, and as you expand the breadth of what you read, you will encounter insights from a range of writers on many subjects that will strike you as genuine gems of language, because they manage to capture the essence of some truth about human nature or some facet of it. Write these down, and don't forget to note the source.

I began my quotation file more than 40 years ago. At the time, I wrote down my discoveries on 3 x 5 index cards, which I then kept in alphabetical order by author in a little green metal box. By current standards that seems quite primitive, but it worked. It really was, however, quite primitive compared to the computerized and eminently searchable treasure I have today. This file is invaluable to me in my writing. Everyone gets mental blocks from time to time. Everyone, no matter how experienced, struggles now and then to understand the essence of an issue or problem. Having recourse to insights that you yourself have collected works to free you from the bonds of your difficulty.

Of course, whole books of quotations exist, divided by author, by subject, and by discipline. The most famous of these is called *Bartlett's Familiar Quotations*, and you should own one of these as well; keep it on a shelf next to your dictionary and your thesaurus. These days, too, one can easily look up, almost instantly, a whole raft of quotations by author or by subject on the internet, and I do not disparage the newer resources we now have at hand. But these instantly produced electronic quotations are not earned. They have not come to us from our own efforts, have not been gleaned from the prose chaff by our own labors, so there is a good chance that we do not really understand them as well as we think we do. Only what we earn becomes truly valuable to us intellectually. There is no other way, sorry.

It takes time to develop one's own quotation file resource. There are detours along the way, too. Something someone said or wrote that you thought was brilliant when you were 18 or 28 may look rather banal when you are 48. But that's fine; one can and one should delete as well as add quotations as time and learning proceed. Since it takes time to develop this resource, you should start today. Of course, just as a person has to put on socks before he can put on shoes, first you will have to read something worthwhile.

Paying careful attention to words and using quotations to hone your conceptual sophistication are very important disciplines to develop. There is one more, however, nearly as important, and it also concerns your capacity to think effectively: Always be attentive to principles of exclusion. Every piece of writing, whether short, medium in length, or long, is limited by its inherent scale. That means you cannot jam all thoughts, all points, all insights into any one piece of writing; as a rule of thumb, the shorter the piece the less you can jam into it. You do not stand a chance of defining what you want to discuss in any given piece of writing unless you also explicitly establish for yourself what you will not discuss. You need not tell the reader what your principles of exclusion are, although there are cases in which you may find it appropriate and useful to do so. The point is that you need to know how to limit yourself, because while stream-of-consciousness thinking is fine for dreams, it is usually not fine for writing.

There are several ways to achieve discipline concerning principles of exclusion. The most common way is to create an outline for what you wish to write, and then stick to it. This is also the most effective way for most writers, so just because you may associate outline writing with some irritating seventh-grade English teacher doesn't mean the teacher was wrong to suggest it. So do it: Make outlines, even for short pieces of writing. Perhaps you will graduate one day from this need, but most likely that date has not yet arrived.

The final general piece of advice I have for you before getting down to specifics about writing is the most important. You must develop internal standards of excellence, by which I mean you must experience the excruciating labors of driving a piece of your own writing to perfection, or as close to perfection as you can get. You will need to do this not once, but several times over a period of months or years. You must develop your own sense of when a piece of writing is really finished. You must learn what you are capable of doing by being able to realize when you have not yet done it.

Isaac Bashevis Singer once said that "the wastepaper basket is the writer's best friend." He was referring to a time before word processors existed, when rewriting and retyping were mandatory, because revisions produced so many scratch-outs, lines, arrows, and white-outs that a text could easily become too convoluted to read. Twenty-first century technology makes such laborious efforts obsolete. Since revisions have become so easy to make, one might think that writers nowadays revise more. But this is not necessarily so. Word processing technology, complete with dozens of fonts and colors and special formats like italics and boldface, makes a piece of writing *look* clean and finished even when it is not. Before word processors, far more time elapsed between drafts. This delay ordained that ideas and prose had to marinate in the author's mind. This did most writers a lot of good. They had no choice but to be patient, for the technology mandated a much slower pace than we have become used to today. This proved an advantage in developing internal standards of excellence.

I came of age at a time before word processing existed, and I therefore have some basis to compare the advantages and disadvantages of the new technology set against the old. That is why, whenever I begin to draft a piece of writing that is particularly important to me, I generally begin with paper and fountain pen. It slows me down. It encourages me to tilt the ratio of thought to drafting toward the former. It helps me not to develop but to maintain in an age of technological temptation my hard-earned internal standards of excellence.

This advice, to develop your own internal standards of excellence, is especially important if younger writers have not been pushed by their teachers or their initial employers to find out what they really can do if they put their minds to it, and to spend the time it takes to get it right. Writing standards in high schools in the United States are abysmal, and in undergraduate college classrooms not much less so. This is because a premium is put on substance, and it is assumed that style and the capacity for clear expression is of secondary concern. There is no time for it. That may be true in some cases, but I frankly doubt it. The result of the bias against taking effective writing seriously is that most young professionals have no idea what they are capable of doing, because no one has ever made them develop internal standards of excellence in writing, and that presupposes in thinking as well. And this means, in turn, that the quality of our political and social discourse as a whole has declined.

There are exceptions, of course, to this decline. A story is told about Henry Kissinger, the American Secretary of State under Presidents Nixon and Ford, when he was still a professor at Harvard University. One of his graduate students, a woman who eventually went on to hold high office in the American government, was obligated at a certain point in her schooling to write a doctoral dissertation prospectus—

essentially a skeletal essay version, stated as a hypothesis, for the book that the dissertation will become. This graduate student worked hard on her prospectus and handed it in to Dr. Kissinger. Several weeks went by and she heard no response, so she called Kissinger and asked what he thought of her prospectus. He answered, "Is this really the best you can do?"

Hearing that response, the student took another look at what she had handed in. She noticed errors of both substance and style that she had overlooked. She quickly prepared a more advanced draft and passed it on to Kissinger with a note of apology. Some weeks passed and again she received no response. Again she called Kissinger, who answered her as before: "Is this really the best you can do?" And so the student reexamined her writing once more, only to find (to her shock and dismay) that still other errors had remained uncorrected and, more important, that a certain sophistication and precision of expression was lacking. And so she prepared a third draft, and once completed handed it in as before. Yet again time passed with no response, and yet again (now for a third time), she called Kissinger to ask his view. Naturally, he replied: "Is this really the best you can do?" And this time—very sincerely and with no little intensity in her voice—the student replied, "Yes, sir, this really is, this time it really, really is, the best that I can do." "Very well, then," said Dr. Kissinger, "now I will read it."

There are several ways to take this story. One is to conclude that Henry Kissinger was an over-the-top sadistic bastard of a dissertation director. Perhaps he was; I did not know him at the time. But I think more generously that the story illustrates a kind of hard love as practiced by a shrewd and effective professor. Dr. Kissinger had already been through the exercise of training graduate students at Harvard many times before he encountered this particular student, and he knew how important it was for students to develop internal standards of excellence. He also knew that simply telling them about it would not do the trick; they had to experience the frustration and do the hard work for themselves.

The general decline in standards of excellence in writing of all kinds is undeniable. However, audiences have not lost all capacity to discern skill where it exists. Write very well and you will push the buttons you aim to push; audiences appreciate quality even if they don't know why. It is an emotional matter, as we discussed in the last chapter. But it is not easy to develop internal standards of excellence. It takes time. It takes a lot of work. It takes a certain character—and a certain respectful orientation to the professional task—to succeed. It helps to be really smart, but being really smart is not enough. As in many walks of life, writing well is a challenge for which humility will get you a lot farther than hubris.

Having set out some very general advice about how to write better, it is now time to be a bit more specific. I will endeavor in what follows in this chapter and the next to do that.

Alas, it is not possible in a short space to cover everything, so I must pick and choose. I am not going to talk about when you should use contractions and when you should avoid them, or about the difference between *it's* and *its*. I am not going to debate the matter of the serial comma, for that is a matter of taste and different generic choices that have been made between the United States and Britain; in this book we use the serial comma. I am not going to tell you when to use a hyphen in an adjectival phrase and when not to, because every style manual explains this clearly. (Hint: Never use one after a word that ends in "ly.") I am not going to tell you never to split an infinitive, because there are times when you can and even should do so. I am not going to point out that poor writers often confuse the meaning of "last" and "past," very often using the former word when they should be using the latter one, or that such writers frequently say "over" such-and-such a number when they mean, and should instead write, "more than." I am not going to stress the importance of transitions between paragraphs, or spend much ink telling you that when you end one paragraph you should avoid pronouns in the first sentence of the next paragraph. All this is simply too obvious to belabor. It's very important, however. Enough said.

Not a word more than what is contained in this paragraph will be spent on explaining that we no longer anthropomorphize nations by using the pronoun "she"—we use "it" instead—and there will be no excessive discussion of when to use abbreviations like U.S. and E.U. (only in an adjectival mode) and when to spell out United States and European Union (always when used as a noun).

Nor am I going to prattle on about the maddening political correctness of gender expression, except to say that, to my way of thinking, having to write "he or she" instead of just "he" or just "she" whenever one wishes to speak generally in the singular tense about something guarantees an awkward sentence. One should not be in the business of writing inevitably awkward sentences, even at the risk of having insecure women (or men, if you always choose "she" instead of "he") imagine that you don't respect them.

Similarly, I will refrain from offering general discourse on the propriety of inserting stock foreign phrases, usually of Latin and French, into your writing. Should you use "as such" or "per se"? Should you use "one thing substituted for another" or "mutatis mutandis"? The basic rule of thumb holds that you avoid foreign loan words and phrases except when they provide genuine economy. Mutatis mutandis and other highfalutin Latin phrases can be problematic to the extent that the average reader may not understand them, but in this case two words beat double that number to make the point. Generally, the more formal the piece of writing the more likely your target readers will be familiar with such terms. You just have to use common sense when in doubt, and I insist on saying no more about this.

Clearly, some choices are matters of taste, as with this business of gender expression, and if your tastes are different from mine, so be it. (It was the Irish playwright George Bernard Shaw who once revised the Golden Rule as follows: "Do not do unto others as you would have them do unto you, because their tastes might be different."[3]) But some choices are not matters of taste: If you write "it's" to indicate a third-person singular pronoun, you have made a mistake, and it matters not how common that mistake has become in recent times. It is still a mistake and, please God, it always will be.

I have chosen to comment on the most common flaws I see and the ones that bother me most; while the two categories overlap considerably, they are not identical. I have also chosen to concentrate on fixing the flaws that will help you the most and bring results the fastest. In short, I have tried to identify some key points that, when followed, can improve your writing. The lack of inclusivity is not a fatal problem, happily, because several excellent manuals of style are out there for everyone to use should they wish to do so. *Fowler's Modern English Usage* is best for most purposes.

Less is more. The most common flaw in writing is a lack of concision. If you really know what you're talking about, you should be able to

---

3. From his play *Man and Superman* (1903).

economize with language, getting right to the point rather than me-
andering all over the page with needless verbiage. Even people who do
seem to know what they're talking about frequently feel compelled to
use five or six words to make the same point that one or two can make
just fine. These are often the same people who think that it is better to
use a longer word then a shorter one that means essentially the same
thing. Maybe in academic writing these inclinations pay off, since
academics often feel status sensitive and go to great lengths to impress
others despite their frequent lack of having anything genuinely new
or interesting to say. But these inclinations don't pay off in political
writing, the kind of writing where the author is trying to persuade the
reader about ideas and policy rather than about the tenure potential
of the author.

The basic idea here is simple: Make it easy for the reader to understand what you are trying to tell him. Do not make the reader work
needlessly to grasp your meaning because readers resent this, and that
does you no good. The reason is, as I have already said, that the human
mind is promiscuously associational. Readers will not give you a break;
if your style is awkward and strews obstacles in the path of their understanding, most will couple their irritation over style with a rejection
of your point. Sometimes readers will simply stop trying, and you are
very unlikely to drive home your point if that happens.

Writing well is difficult, especially for novices. But even experienced
writers typically go through eight or 10 or 12 drafts of an essay before
it meets their internal standard of excellence. This is what led the
novelist Peter de Vries to remark: "I love being a writer. What I can't
stand is the paperwork."

Different writers have different methods of getting to the finish line,
but overwhelmingly the drafting process is one in which self-indulgent
and lazy language is tightened repeatedly into more focused, more
precise, and more concise expression. You can replace a phrase like "she
did not have" with "she lacked" and halve the number of words you
need to say the same thing. This is a capillary-level example of less is
more, but punctilious editing—of your own work as well as that of
others—can often do even better, using one or two words in place of
six, eight, or ten. Taken by themselves, such little improvements may
not seem efficacious, but taken together they can and usually do make
a huge difference in the quality of any piece of writing. Concision in
writing is the rough equivalent of Occam's razor—simplicity—in logic

and argument: Do not multiply factors beyond necessity. It is true in writing no less than in logic; parsimony is beautiful.

Of course, as with most things, one can go too far. The opposite of verbosity is excessive density. It is possible to condense language beyond prudence, leaving readers not with the clear but the cryptic. Sometimes the proper thing to do is to concretize abstract language with examples, and that will necessarily mean adding words to an otherwise desiccated text. For most fledgling writers, however, this is rarely a problem.

If you would like a rule here, then remind yourself repeatedly as you are editing your own work that every word must carry water.[4] Every word must have a purpose in conveying your meaning or in creating the emotional pitch you seek. If a word doesn't do that, out it goes. If you know this from the start, then you will, in time, be able to write concisely from the get-go, thus reducing the amount of subsequent editing you will need to do. The reward is as simple as the rule: less is more in the sense that an experienced writer can use fewer words to accomplish greater ends, and do it faster than an inexperienced writer.

Know your purpose, and your audience. Every piece of writing, whether it is devoted to political persuasion or not, has some purpose outside of the writer's need for self-expression. Even writers of fiction and poetry who simply feel compelled to get whatever it is that's bothering them off their chests still have readers in mind when they do so. They had better, if they want to be successful, keep their readers, and make a living. Knowing one's purpose is joined at the hip with your intended audience. You cannot answer the question of what you seek to accomplish with any given piece of writing unless you know with respect to whom you wish to accomplish it. Not all audiences are created equal, and you must be able to discern relevant differences among them.

What is worse, you may face what is called the multiple-audience problem, which goes as follows: You may wish to address one particular audience but other audiences may overhear you. This is not a particularly acute problem in general writing, but it is a nasty problem in political writing, and especially in speechwriting undertaken on behalf of high

---

4. A good, stiff lecture on this point, very much worth your time, is George Orwell's classic 1946 essay "Politics and the English Language." Its text can be found easily through an internet search; see, for instance, george-orwell.org.

government officials. (We will return to the multiple-audience problem in Chapter 7, where we discuss speechwriting in more detail.)

It is not always easy to define one's purpose, especially at the outset of a writing project. Writing is in some respects a form of thinking launched into the general flux of conversational noise, so that the process of writing doubles back on your thinking. Your purpose may change as you delve deeper into a writing project. That is understandable and in many cases laudable. There is a lot to be said for flexibility. Nonetheless, you must still have some idea of your purpose—and its target audience—before you start. If you don't, you will be guilty of some variety of free association, which can be fun but which rarely constitutes the most efficient way to communicate with others unless those others have simply enormous amounts of time on their hands, and are very forgiving sorts of people.

Sentence art. Uncountable are the number of books and essays that have been written over the years about sentences—how to appreciate them, how to write them, and how to rewrite them. Most of this advice concerns writing as an art form rather than as a persuasive instrument; but, when the advice is good advice, it applies to all forms of writing. One can overdo it, though, because a sentence is only an intermediate structure in language. Sentences depend on words and phrases to the one side, and, of course, they are embedded in paragraphs on the other side. As no man is an island, neither is a sentence. Think of a sentence as a tooth. A tooth is a useful thing. But two teeth are more useful, and even better is a whole mouthful of them. Teeth work best in organized ensemble form, and so do sentences. Let your mind chew on that for a while.

That said, some standard advice about sentence construction is nevertheless worth passing on. Several excellent writers who have at one point or another turned their minds to method have suggested that fine sentences should not begin or end with weak words. This is good advice, again, so long as it is not overdone. Such advice also helps explain the prohibition against ending sentences with prepositions, for no preposition is a strong word. Here's an example of a strong sentence, in this case from the King James translation of the Hebrew Bible: "Vengeance is mine, sayeth the Lord." "Vengeance" is definitely not a weak word, and neither is "Lord." That is one heckuva sentence. But suppose for a moment that God (or Moses, depending on your theology) had been a poor writer and had let loose with something like this instead: "It is vengeance that is mine, I, the Lord, wish to say to you." "It is" is made up of two weak words, and "wish to say to you" could not lift a hummingbird feather even if all five words concerted their strength.

So yes, it is true: Sentences that begin with locutions such as "There are" or "It is" are liable to be weak sentences. This does not mean you cannot or should not use them, for every sentence need not be and should not be strong. Just as sentence construction should be mindful of how to emphasize the most important word components within it, so paragraphs need be constructed to emphasize the most important sentences within them. If all the sentences in a paragraph are strong ones, none will stand out, resulting in a paragraph sans contrast. That's much better than a paragraph made up of all weak sentences, to be sure, but it is still not best, or even good.

Much of the sound advice that has come down to us about sentence art concerns matters of order and emphasis. In simple sentences, generally identifiable as those not requiring commas, concern with order and emphasis is also a simple matter. The most common form of an English sentence is one that starts with the noun, moves immediately to the verb and closes by naming some object. So, for example, "Johnny threw the ball." The reader knows right away what is important here. This sentence is about Johnny. The reader quickly finds out what Johnny did; he threw something. And no moss is going to grow under the feet of that reader while he learns what got thrown. It was a ball. But if you start mucking around, as writers will, with sentences that have two, three, or more components or phrases, then you have choices as to which components to put in which order.

The sentence I just wrote is a good example. I could have written that sentence as follows: "You have choices in sentences that have two, three, or more components or phrases as to their placement and order, if you muck around with such sentences, as writers will do." Or I could have written it a third, and possibly even a fourth way just by rearranging the order of the sentence's component parts, adjusting grammatically as necessary. Sometimes it is quite clear that one choice of order is better than others—for example, when a certain order accentuates the word concepts abiding in either the verb or the noun that you prefer to emphasize. If the sentence buries the words that are most important to its meaning and purpose, forcing the reader to work to identify them, then most likely that sentence is poorly ordered. Sometimes, however, one choice of ordering will seem as good as another. In cases like that, your judgment should turn on how that particular sentence fits in with its resident paragraph.

Some who would tender advice to young writers propose a particular exercise. The exercise adjures the writer to search for strong sentences, to map out their structure, and then to substitute new words for old ones. Suppose we say that the sentence "Vengeance is mine, sayeth the Lord" is a good model of a strong sentence, and we set about using its structure, adjusted a bit to edit out the antiquish "sayeth," to produce a new sentence. We could write, for example, "Victory is mine, proclaims the great salt sea" after a great wave sinks some hubristic captain with his boat. That works.

Another example: "Nationalism is for me the expression of collective liberty and the condition of individual liberty."[5] That is a very good, very strong sentence. It begins with a strong word and it ends with two strong words. It is complex in meaning yet needs no comma, let alone any underlining or italics, nearly always a sign of a strong sentence. Now let's tamper with it. "Liberalism is for us the vanguard of a just society and the creed of each individual conscience." That works, too (especially if you are a Democrat).

So this exercise can be useful, at least until the art of sentence structure becomes second nature to you. But it is not, as some claim, a silver bullet, the be-all and end-all of writing instruction.[6] You cannot take an entire essay, let alone a whole book, and go through replacing the original's nouns, verbs, and objects with those that suit your own design. Well, you could, but it would be an extremely tedious task. More important, in order for such tedium actually to be useful to you en masse, you would have to make a match emotionally and in terms of purpose between the original and your substituted version. That seems like vastly more trouble than it is worth. In small doses, however, this writing medicine does some good; hence, the writing assignment that attends this chapter.

Speaking of commas, as we did a moment ago, here is another pointer for you. In complex sentences it is natural for components or phrases to be set off by couplets of commas. That is as it must be, but sentences are typically improved by removing comma couplets. For example, I

---

5. See *Job's Dungheap* (New York: Schocken Books, 1948), p. 70.
6. So claims, for example, Stanley Fish in *How to Write a Sentence and How to Read One* (New York: Harper, 2011).

can write: "Last night, it seems to me, was a colossal waste of time." Or I can write: "It seems to me that last night was a colossal waste of time." Which is the better sentence? All else equal, the one without the comma couplet is the better sentence. But all is rarely equal. The inferior sentence might turn into the superior one depending on the context of the paragraph into which it fits. Still, you should make a habit of going through your writing looking for ways to consolidate language by eliminating gratuitous comma couplets. It will help you on your quest to implement the imperative of less is more.

Sentence lengths and forms. Now that you have some sense of sentences, let us look to how sentences are combined. Another very common frailty of mediocre writing is that it fails to vary sentence lengths and forms. Language is inherently musical, especially in oral form but also, by association, in writing. It has rhythm; it has cadence. The emotional vector of language is partly contained in its rhythm. If evolutionary biologists are to be believed, humankind probably sang before speaking and danced before walking. If you wish to engage your readers and bring them along with you, appeal to the inherent musicality sensed in the listening and in the reading of all articulate speech.

Different languages have different ways of expressing themselves. Some are more limited than others. But English is extraordinarily rich, both in the vocabulary it offers and in the variability of style it allows. The reason for this is that the contemporary English language represents the confluence of three major language families: Romance languages via Latin and Old French mainly, Teutonic languages via Old English, and Greek. We English speakers and writers are very lucky in this, but luck carries with it a responsibility to make good use of our resources. Dispensing that responsibility when writing the English language means varying lengths and styles the same way a composer would when creating symphonies or sonatas. Certain patterns can repeat, but if the same pattern always repeats, the result is a tedious and unskilled composition. It is the same in writing.

If all or nearly all of your sentences are roughly the same length, you are writing poorly. It doesn't matter if all of them are short, which gives writing a kind of staccato feel, or if all of them are very long. Both are sins of English composition.

Now again, a fine line often divides good advice from matters of taste in writing over which honest and intelligent people may differ. Some writers of fiction have succeeded grandly by writing altogether too many short, staccato-like sentences for my taste. Ernest Hemingway was one, and J.D. Salinger was another. When one is trying to capture the voice or the dialect of characters in fiction, as Salinger did in his famous book *Catcher in the Rye*, this kind of writing can work well enough. It can convey a certain kind of personality, someone who is either gruff or distressed or old or tired. In general, however, in nonfiction writing you would be wise to avoid playing around with staccato, lest you convey gruffness, distress, old age, or exhaustion when you do not mean to do so.

Similarly, if you always or very frequently begin your sentences with throat clearing prepositional language, using words and phrases such as "In fact," "However," "Nevertheless," "Of course," and so forth, you are writing poorly. It is fine to use such words and phrases sometimes (although, as we will soon see, it is not all right to use the phrase "In fact," except very sparingly), as I do here. Just don't overuse them.

If all or nearly all of your sentences start with the sentence's noun, you may be writing clearly but you are also writing poorly. If you find in reviewing a piece of writing that all or nearly all of your verbs are simple present tense and none or virtually none are expressed as present participles—and similarly, if you are always using the simple past instead of past participles—something is wrong, or at least less than optimal and easily improvable.

Fortunately, you can check rather easily for all of these flaws. All you have to do is go back over your writing with these pitfalls in mind. When you see something systematically wrong with a piece of writing, you must then redraft it with an ear for rhythm and cadence. There is nothing wrong with putting substance before style in your writing. Once you've conveyed your substance, however, it is time to edit your writing for style. Style should never be so late an afterthought that it occurs to you when it is too late to do anything about it.

Paragraph intelligence. Just as sentences can be drafted in such a way as to make your writing seem tedious, so the division of writing into paragraphs affects both rhythm and cadence. Punctuation breathes the life of oral language into our writing, of which more in Chapter 3. The same goes for carefully crafted paragraphs.

Just as the overall structure of an expertly designed musical composition reflects the skillful balancing of its parts, so a piece of writing must have an overall structure in which the parts are balanced to make a proper whole. The division of paragraphs is designed to indicate when one integral thought stops and another is set to begin. That is perfectly true; but that is not the only thing that paragraph divisions do. Always nearby the objective function of language in communication is the emotional function, so that if all of your paragraphs are about the same length, even if that division accords well with the objective logic of the piece, you have forfeited a chance to make your writing more attractive, more enticing to the reader.

Moreover, a reader's eyes will take in a whole page of writing at once. Seeing very long paragraphs can be off-putting. It conveys to a reader that the challenge before him is time-consuming and difficult. Seeing a series of very short paragraphs may convey to a reader that what is before him is not serious, and hence possibly not worth the time it would take to read it. When the eyes see paragraphs of varying lengths, the most likely effect is to invite curiosity and investigation. You probably never realized that a piece of writing can have characteristics similar to that of a presentational symbol, like a painting. But it can.

Look at this page as a whole, as though it were a presentational symbol. Notice how the paragraph lengths differ. Now flip through the book at random and alight your eyes on any page where I have made less of a conscious effort to vary paragraph length, and what do you see? Which pages looks more interesting, all else equal?

Subheads and titles. What is true of paragraph intelligence is also true for the use of subheads and other means of dividing text to make it more assimilable to the reader. Some editors and writers do not like subheads. They believe that a text should be written so skillfully that the logical flow of the writing itself obviates the need for what they consider to be gimmicks. I admire that trust in the potential skill of writers, and I concur with the essence of the judgment. But let us be practical: Few writers can carry that off, and even fewer readers have patience for those writers who cannot. One should not break up the text too much, just as one should not break it up too little. This is, in other words, a Goldilocks problem, as in neither too hot nor too cold, too hard nor too soft, too high nor too low. (So much of life is, you know.) I have dealt with the dilemma in this book through a compromise: this chapter and the next excepted, I have broken up the text with what are called "drop caps"—large boldfaced letters starting off chapter sections. You have already seen several of them, and your computer probably has a way for you to use them, as well, even if you have not yet become aware of it.

If you do use them, subheads should be thought of as opportunities, not merely as signposts and certainly not as gimmicks. They offer the writer an opportunity to condense a great deal of meaning into just a few words, and they entice readers into following the flow of an argument that might otherwise overwhelm or elude them.

What is true of subheads goes double for titles. Usually an editor, not an author, has the final word concerning titles, but an author has to suggest one when the submission goes forward. If a title is good enough, it will not only help sell the piece to the editor, it might even stick if the editor cannot think of anything better. So pay close attention to titles, and work to come up with truly excellent ones.

In this regard, let me conclude this piece of advice with a very important directive: Never, ever call the beginning of an essay an introduction. Even more important, never, ever call the end of an essay a conclusion. It is obvious even to a third grader that the beginning of an essay is the introduction and that the end of it is, or at least ought to be, some kind of conclusion. You don't have to tell readers this, any more than you need to hand them a ball peen hammer with directions to clobber themselves at certain intervals in order to grasp your points. Worse, by calling sections of an essay names that are already obvious to everyone you waste opportunities to drive home your argument.

As a general rule, too, there is no point in putting a subhead before the beginning of a piece of writing, except in a book, where some kind of preface or forward is needed. In a book, too, you can use "introduction" to name the beginning section. Each chapter within a book should begin under its title directly, with no subhead whatsoever, and certainly with no chapter subhead saying "Introduction."

Writer's block. Many people complain of writer's block. Few are sure what exactly it is, but they complain about it anyway. Writer's block is what led Gene Fowler, the legendary editor of the *Baltimore Sun* in its heyday, to say: "Writing is easy. All you do is sit staring at a blank sheet of paper until the drops of blood form on your forehead." Know the feeling? So what is writer's block exactly, and how does one overcome it?

There are several sources of writer's block and, unfortunately, nothing you have learned so far in this chapter can be counted upon to keep the condition at bay. One source is sheer unadulterated terror. Deadlines have a nasty tendency to evoke such terror. The average human being, and in particular the average young American, is a natural-born procrastinator. Writing assignments have a tendency to paralyze students, sending them to bowling alleys, bars, and shopping malls with abandon. Eventually, these individuals will cop a look at the calendar, see that a paper is due to some stodgy professor by a date certain, make a kind of a plan to get the work done, fail to execute the plan, and then, just a few days before the assignment is due, go stark raving crazy. The emotional turmoil of impending doom can so raise the body's primitive fight-or-flight reaction that dispassionate skills acquired in pain and self-sacrifice at writing the English language go the way of residual chicken bones, stale salsa, and warm beer. In short, our hero is screwed, and this he calls "writer's block."

That is only one way to define writer's block, however. Less dramatically, the most common reason for writer's block is that the would-be writer has not yet thought through the subject matter sufficiently to know how to master the next step, which is communicating something to others. The entire topic floats like a fog of disorganized ambiguity in the aching brain of the would-be author. Nothing comes clear. There is no first sentence in the offing, nor any outline in prospect. And all the while the clock is ticking down to the hour of doom. We have said it before, and we may say it yet again: If you can't think straight, you can't write well.

But suppose, just for the sake of illustration, that the writer in question actually has done the necessary preparatory work for the writing assignment, whether this assignment be ensconced in a school or be part of an initiatory professional position. And still, our would-be author cannot find his muse. It happens. It may not happen to everyone, but it happens a lot. What should you do about it if it happens to you?

Actually, a large menu of options awaits the needy. If people were not so much in a state of panic and sizzling incandescent fear, they would readily think of these options themselves. But they are, so they don't. Hence what follows.

One way to get yourself on track if you find yourself blocked is to turn away from the keyboard, pick up a pen and a piece of paper, and set to write the old-fashioned way. Sometimes your problem isn't that the words aren't coming, it's that they are coming too fast for you to handle. You need to slow yourself down, stop trying to drink out of your own fire-hose—a condition that is much encouraged, by the way, by the nature and pace of the internet. You can't write if you can't hear what's in your own head.

Sometimes all it takes to find your muse is a good nap, a walk outside where the vistas are wide, or a stiff bolt of single malt. Sometimes you must go the extra mile, and one method for that hike is to speak your ideas into an audio recording device of some kind, take a break, play back what you have recorded and transcribe it as you listen. Some people are flat amazed at what this fiddling with modalities can do for their confidence and creativity.

An even simpler and yet effective way to conquer writer's block is to seek the help of a friend. Just talk to a friend, and let that friend say back to you what she thought she just heard you say. Your ideas coming out of the mouth of an intelligent other can make a world of difference. Try it; you'll see.

Recommended Reading

George Orwell, "Politics and the English Language" (1946), in *A Collection of Essays* (Boston, MA: Houghton Mifflin Harcourt, 1970).

Robert Nisbet, "Metaphor" and "Wit," in *Prejudices: A Philosophical Dictionary* (Cambridge, MA: Harvard University Press, 1983).

"George S. Kaufman," in Jon Winokur, ed., *The Portable Curmudgeon* (New York: Plume, 1992).

Writing Exercise

Find a copy of John Barth's 1960 epic colonial American novel *The Sot-Weed Factor* and read up to p. 17. (A free download of the text is available through the Internet Archive at http://www.archive.org/details/sotweedfactor006326mbp.) Once you have a feel for Barth's style, take p. 18 and systematically transform it—sentence by sentence, phrase by phrase—into a page from your own not-yet-written autobiography. Maintain exactly Barth's syntax as you go, substituting your own substance as much as you can, so that you replace as much as possible of Barth's original. Stop when you get to the bottom of the page. (Then finish reading the novel; you won't regret it.)

3 WRITING BETTER STILL

Now that we have covered some key general aspects of how to write well, we need to dig down into more specific matters—17 of them, to be exact—before we can move on to address the various forms of persuasive, political writing.

Tenses and tone. A ubiquitous sign of weak writing is the specter of inconsistent verb tenses. A bad piece of writing may start in the present tense and without warning flip to simple past and then back again to the present tense. Even worse, a piece of writing may start in the future tense with the author's claims about what is to come, only to lurch suddenly into the past tense, then into the present, only to come back at the end to the future. Of course, depending on what a writer is talking about, verb tenses can and should change. But they should not change randomly. Many times in an immature piece of writing, a skilled editor can see right away how conditional tenses can ease a problem of this kind. If a writer does not know whether to use present or past tense, sometimes using the past perfect tense fixes the problem. It should, because that's what it's for.

As a rule, *set-up language* in the future tense at the top of any piece of writing is a bad idea. It suggests to the perspicacious reader that the author is winging it; if the piece were really finished, the author would have already done what was promised, so the proper tense to use is present tense. That projects much more confidence to the reader. It tells the reader that what he is spending time on is not a whim but a done deal.

While I am at it, let me note to that set-up language should be kept to a minimum. Sometimes it is necessary, especially at the beginning of a long and complex argument. But most unseasoned writers wildly overdo this kind of thing. Just let the argument speak for itself whenever possible.

Just as one should keep a close watch on consistency with verb tenses, so one should keep a close watch on one's tone. If you begin a piece of writing in a serious mien, keep it serious. If you start out with a lighter sensibility, take care not to shift gears abruptly. A master writer on occasion can mix tones effectively, depending on how that writer wishes to drag a reader into and out of a range of emotion. But if a writer is going to do this kind of high wire act with tone, it has to be carefully deliberate. Most of the time when one sees variations in tone in a piece of writing, it is a function of indiscipline, not any special skill.

Passive voice. Next to excessive and pointless loquacity, the use of passive voice in sentence construction is the most ubiquitous sin in poor writing. It really should not be necessary for me to define what I mean by "passive voice" construction, but since the teaching of English in American high schools has fallen on such hard times, I feel I must. Indeed, I know from eavesdropping on the experience of my three children—each of whom went to supposedly excellent high schools—that English grammar is barely taught at all anymore. Very few students have any idea what the parts of speech are before they encounter them in the process of learning a foreign language, and very few have ever seen a sentence diagrammed. Possibly, some of you reading this paragraph right now don't even know what I mean by sentence diagramming. This is sad, but be that as it may, let us get down to business.

Consider this sentence: "Johnny threw the baseball through the plate glass window." That is active voice. "Johnny" is the noun, and "threw" is the verb. "The baseball" is the direct object and the rest of the sentence may also be identified in terms of parts of speech, but for our purposes in defining passive voice the rest is not important. Now consider this sentence: "The baseball was thrown through the plate glass window by Johnny." This is passive voice. Instead of "Johnny" being the noun, "the baseball" is the noun. Instead of "threw" being the verb, "was thrown" is the verb phrase.

Notice the general effect of passive voice: It eliminates the identification of the actual agent of the action. A passive voice sentence is without question grammatically correct; it is a full sentence with noun and verb. But it also constitutes basic fraud. It is elusive. It is deceptive. It ultimately confuses to the reader, who cannot be blamed for losing track of who's doing what to whom. Passive voice is nearly always a sign of bad writing, especially when such sentences literally litter the page. Professional editors are very sensitive to passive voice. A large chunk of what they do when they fix the English of other writers involves turning sentences around from passive to active voice.

Now, passive voice construction is not always bad. There are times, after all, when hiding the identity of the active agent in a behavior is exactly what a writer wishes to do. Deception is the order of the day in such cases; it aligns with the purpose of the writing in the first place. Such purposes are ubiquitous in political writing. When you see passive voice in political writing, especially writing undertaken by public officials, you can bet your bottom dollar someone is trying to hide something. I will leave it to your imagination to figure out why. But let a trivial example illustrate the point.

One of my students scored a summer internship in Congress a few years back. One of her jobs was to answer the phone (in other words, to be the receptionist). Occasionally, she would lose a call by pushing a wrong button. When the Congressman's staff director confronted her about this, she replied not that, "I'm sorry I lost the calls," but rather, "The calls were lost, I am sorry to say." You see the difference. They gave her another job anyway.

The documentary tense. Next to the prolific use of passive voice, nothing depresses a good writer or a good editor so much as the excessive use of what I call the documentary tense. Technically speaking, I am referring to a perfectly legitimate verb tense called the future perfect. An example of a sentence using this tense goes something like this: "When Charlie was a boy he spent many hours on the river, an experience that would make him an excellent nature guide decades later."

There is nothing wrong with that sentence. The problem with this tense comes when it is used inappropriately and excessively, as it invariably is in those extremely irritating British sports documentaries where the moderator is always speaking in hushed tones about some dramatic achievement in the making. These things are so bad that the genre has become a popular source for ridicule and lampooning. (If you do not know what I am referring to, you are in for a real treat.)

About 98 percent of the time that the documentary tense is invoked in mediocre writing, what is really called for is the simple past or, on some occasions, the past perfect. When the future perfect, or documentary, tense is overused, it becomes impossible to sustain drama. Why? Because nothing especially dramatic is happening. This makes a piece of writing sound artificially breathless, pandemonic, and downright silly. The future perfect tense is used correctly only about 2 percent of the time; the other 98 percent should be lined up against a wall and shot—with a delete key, of course.

Sentence fragments. A paragraph later on in this chapter contains the sentence fragment: "Or not." There is no obvious noun and there is certainly no verb there. What is the rule concerning sentence fragments?

The first thing you need to know, rule or no rule, is how to distinguish between a sentence and a sentence fragment. Nearly everyone knows that to be a sentence the words strung together must have a noun and a verb, but that is not good enough as a definition because strings of words can contain nouns and verbs within and still not constitute a grammatical sentence. I once asked a group of English teachers to give me a concise and infallible definition of a sentence fragment, and they could not do it. Their answer came down to a paraphrase of Supreme Court justice Potter Stewart's definition of pornography, which is simply that one knows it (both a real sentence and a dirty picture) when one sees it.

Perhaps that used to be true, but it is true no longer. The average undergraduate native English speaker cannot distinguish a sentence from a sentence fragment any more than he can distinguish Jägermeister from cough syrup in a blind test. I think we can do a little bit better than that. You have a sentence when you can find the noun and the verb that constitute the irreducible essence of meaning, but which are not contained within a noun phrase (such a phrase usually starting with the word *which* or *that*).

Once you know the difference between a grammatical sentence and a sentence fragment, the rule is, don't use sentence fragments. Every once in a while, of course, you can get away with a fragment quip and the world will not come to an end. But sentence fragments should be deployed very sparingly. In very formal writing, they should not be used at all.

The reason for bringing this up in the first place is that Americans live today in a verbal environment at large that is heavily polluted with advertising language, and the need for concision when writing on Twitter and Facebook isn't helping either. A lot of people not only cannot distinguish between a grammatical sentence and a sentence fragment, they just don't care one way or the other. And the advertising copywriters know that they don't know and don't care, and so it appears that they don't care even more.

An example: A few weeks ago I noticed for the first time a sign in the Washington Metro that read exactly as follows, with white letters on a dark blue background: "Now you don't need a Metrorail farecard machine or Metrobus farebox to add value. All you need is a computer and an online SmarTrip account with Metro. Simply log onto MetroOpensDoors.com and add value from your credit card. Loading value online. It's the smartest thing to happen to riding Metro since SmarTrip itself!"

Not only is it easy to spot the sentence fragment here, it is easy to see that simply putting a colon after the fragment instead of a period would have fixed the copy grammatically, and that none of the emphasis in the ad would have been lost as a result. So why did Metro write it this way? Was it deliberate for some unknown reason, or did these people not know what a sentence fragment is or realize that it is grammatically incorrect? I asked. The answer I got suggested the latter, and also that these folks couldn't care less. Words matter; standards matter—and in such domains the alternative to high standards is not low standards but no standards.

The American political environment is not exempt from the general trend of substituting the advertising mentality for one described best as a professional planning attitude. I can't see that this trend has done the quality of the American political conversation any good. This is one reason why I am not a fan of PowerPoint, which has become almost obligatory in U.S. government and military circles. It is possible, and I have seen it done in a U.S. military context, to use this technology effectively. But most of the time PowerPoint carries only sentence fragments, and it is in the nature of a sentence fragment, where noun and verb are never joined together in holy meaning, that coherent thoughts cannot be expressed. Never mind the distraction PowerPoint presentations cause in pulling attention away from a speaker, and never mind the demobilization caused by the dimming of the lights necessary to see the screen on which the presentation is projected. This technology, as it is typically used, has the general effect of disorganizing our stock of knowledge about any given subject.

The stranded "however." However is a fine word most of the time. It is an ever so slightly upscale version of *but,* when you think about it. But it is not fine all of the time, and it is particularly not fine when the word is found stranded in the middle of a sentence where it never should have been allowed to wander in the first place. A surefire sign of not just mediocre but downright bad writing is the presence the "stranded *however.*"

Now, what do we mean by the "stranded *however*"? The best place to look for examples are in signs meant to instruct the public in one way or another, but one finds them often enough in actual writing as well. Here is an example from a hospital: "Visiting hours are from 10 AM to 9 PM Monday through Thursday, however, they are from noon to 11 PM on Fridays and the weekend." This is a use of the word *however* that indicates a writer who does not know how to use either a period or a semicolon. This is a writer who resembles a driver who loses control of his car and panics momentarily before regaining mastery. During the panic, a driver is liable to do most anything. A writer just sticks in the word *however* and moves on.

Let's go back and fix the offending sentence about visiting hours. Let us fix it first with a period. "Visiting hours are from 10 AM to 9 PM Monday through Thursday. They are from noon to 11 PM on Fridays and the weekend." Now let's fix it with a semicolon. "Visiting hours are from 10 AM to 9 PM Monday through Thursday; they are from noon to 11 PM on Fridays and the weekend." We can fix it even better without using a semicolon: "Visiting hours are from 10 AM to 9 PM Monday through Thursday, noon to 11 PM on Friday and the weekend." See how easy that is? No more stranded *however.* Good riddance.

The naked "it." Another common flaw of mediocre or immature writing is that one encounters what may be referred to as the "naked *it*" all over the page. Clearly, the word *it* is a pronoun that always refers back to some noun. We know what the word *it* means from context, or at least we are supposed to know what it means from context. We don't know what it means when the context is so screwed up, convoluted, or obscured by bad writing that we cannot figure out the referent. Most commonly, this problem rears its ugly head in the form of two possibilities as to what "it" might refer to, but without any definite tip-off as to which possibility is the right or intended one.

There is no secret as to why this happens. You the writer know what you're talking about. The subject is familiar to you, presumably, or you would not be writing about it. You have thought about it, if not a lot, then at least very likely more than the reader. It is your train of thought for which you are laying down track in writing, so you know what *it* refers to so well that you assume your readers will know, too. They often won't. So you need to go *it* hunting as you edit your own work, reading "defensively" to protect your readers from frustration and gratuitous work. Given the wonders of technology, this task is much easier today than it used to be. You can simply set up your computer to search for *it* so that you can satisfy yourself that every time it appears the referent is clear. Do it. (That little sentence is a double entendre, in case you missed "it.")

While we are speaking of third-person pronouns, note a different, more politically salient phenomenon I call the "anonymous *they.*" The third-person plural pronoun "they" can also lose its referent, just like *it.* Over the past two or three decades, I have noticed a significant uptick in the use of the word *they* at the beginning of sentences—more in speech than in writing—with no referent whatsoever anywhere in sight. Usually referring to some troublesome or nefarious groups of people the speaker can't really identify, such sentences can go like this: "They don't know what to do about the economy." "They should intervene to stop the killing of protesters in Syria." "They know the truth about 9/11." Alarmingly, the use of the "anonymous *they*" frequently substitutes for what should be *we,* as though the speaker or writer is distancing himself from a political community of which he is a self-alienated part. The problem with the anonymous *they* usually isn't a simple usage error but rather an indication that the speaker is less than six degrees of separation away from a conspiracy theory.

Go "which" hunting. While you are hunting for wayward uses of *it,* you might as well take Strunk & White's advice to go *which* hunting at the same time. Any manual of style worth its salt will be able to clarify for you the difference between the words *that* and *which.* I'm not going to repeat the distinction here except to say that *that* indicates a general object or category to come in the sentence, while *which* indicates a more specific elaboration or identification within a general category already stated or implied. I simply want to point out two things.

First, there is a difference between British and American English when it comes to the uses of the word *which.* The British use the word almost interchangeably with *that,* and this is the one case where British usage is inferior to American usage. Second, the tendency among mediocre writers of American English is to use *which* instead of *that* when it follows a plural noun, and the other way around when it follows a singular noun. There is absolutely no justification for this whatsoever, and I am mystified by how this pattern of error arose. The general rule of thumb: When in doubt, always use *that* except after a comma, which indicates (see?) that *which* will nearly always be the right choice.

There is, however, a slight complication worth noting. Sometimes a sentence can be so complex that the word *that* will appear twice, or will want to appear twice in close proximity. The second *that* in such a sentence sounds terribly awkward most of the time, and so it is permissible to use *which* in place of the second *that*. By way of example, you might write a sentence like this: "The last time that a full moon that rose so red happened in springtime, I was a young man." If you do write a sentence like that, you should change it to read: "The last time that a full moon which rose so red happened in springtime, I was a young man." Better still, as I say, don't write sentences like that at all. In this case, you can just get rid of the first *that* altogether and switch the *which* back to *that,* and you'll be a lot better off. Any sentence that "wants" to use the word *that* twice is a sentence *that/which* is usually best rewritten—including this one.

While we are discussing the difference between *that* and *which,* we might as well address the difference between *that* and *who* so you are sure to get them completely straight. Consider this sentence: "The gentleman *that* came over from Ohio stole the pumpkin." No. That's wrong. "The gentleman *who* came over from Ohio stole the pumpkin" may not mean a whole heck of a lot to you, but it is at least grammatically correct. *Who* refers back to people, while *that* refers back to things, animate and not. No one should be allowed to graduate from an American high school without knowing this, but these days it is nevertheless a very common error.

Punctuation. All of the conventions of punctuation are designed ultimately to infuse written language with the dynamism of actual human speech. Punctuation tells readers when to breathe. And of course, in so doing, punctuation is a form of politeness. It implicitly tells the reader that the writer cares about him.[1] Punctuation thus has the power to convey empathy, and the really amazing thing about it is that it can convey empathy not only across space but through time. When we read the fine prose of authors long since dead, they somehow come back to life: We can hear their voices, and thanks to punctuation we can even hear them breathing.

---

1. On this underappreciated point, see Lynne Truss, *Eats, Shoots & Leaves* (London: Profile Books, 2003).

Punctuation conventions are to some extent arbitrary, and they do change. If you examine English literature from a few centuries ago, you will see what strikes us as a curiously prolific use of commas. At other periods in English literature you will find almost no commas at all. This is probably not because people actually spoke the English language differently at different times in terms of rhythm and cadence. It likely has more to do with the arbitrary conventions of schoolteachers. But whatever the rules happen to be, you should follow them.

This is not the place to exhaust all the rules of placing commas; that is why there are style guides, and that is why you should buy one and use it. The key to comma usage is to make your written language sound the way it would if you were speaking it. Now go back to the first sentence in this paragraph for just a moment and look at the words after the semicolon. As you can see, I put a comma after the word *guides.* I did not have to do this; the sentence would have been quite proper without it. But I put it there because I wanted to emphasize the second part of the phrase. I made you breathe after that comma, so that your attention was renewed just in advance of the advice I wanted you to take. When we speak, and when we listen, we pick up all sorts of subtle cues. When we write, we are relatively impoverished in this regard. But the skillful use of punctuation redeems that impoverishment at least to some extent.

The point, therefore, is not only that you must learn proper punctuation from a technical point of view—knowing the difference between a semicolon and a colon, for example—but that you must understand punctuation for its more sophisticated purposes. And to think, a few minutes ago you probably did not realize that there were any.

Semicolons. We'll begin by clarifying what a semicolon actually is and what it does. This relatively rare punctuation mark is actually quite handy if you know how to use it. Any decent style guide, like *Fowler's Modern English Usage* or Strunk & White's justly famous guide, *The Elements of Style,* will supply a good definition. For our purposes, however, the easiest way to understand the semicolon is to think of it as dividing one integral thought into two parts. The second part, after the punctuation, almost invariably adds something to or qualifies the first part. In combination, both parts make up a complete thought. It is possible to do the same thing in two distinct sentences, and there are editors whose tastes run against the semicolon. But there is something elegant about the semicolon when used properly, and you will note that mastering it will help you to vary your sentence lengths. Had you written a short sentence, and then followed with two more short sentences expressing a single idea, you would have three short sentences in a row. Not good. If you combine the latter two sentences into one using a semicolon, you are much better off.

So if that is what a semicolon does, what does a colon do? It does two main things. First, it can set off a list. You can write, for example, "The grocery order was extensive on the breakfast side of things: eggs, butter, cheese, and milk." Second and more interestingly, it can tee up an example of a general statement, as, for example, "The best things in life are free: Being true to one's conscience is therefore the greatest freedom of all." When a colon is used in this latter fashion, and when what follows the colon is itself a complete sentence, one usually capitalizes the first word, just as one would in any sentence. A special example of the latter case is the use of a colon to set up a quote: "Imagine some quote in here, please, because that makes my point." Thank you.

Try not to mix up these two punctuation marks, please. If you're not clear on the distinction between a semicolon and a colon as I have explained and illustrated it, then by all means consult *Fowler's*. It never fails.

Parentheses and em-dashes. Students often want to know when to use parentheses to bury some comment within one's own composition, and when the far more exotic em-dash should be used. This is a relatively new question because it reflects a new problem both in the sense that the em-dash is itself a relatively new invention as far as English composition goes, and that it is much abused and overused.

The simplest answer to this question is that you use parentheses when the content within those parentheses is logically subordinate to or merely elaborative of the text it deigns to modify. The set of em-dashes, on the other hand, operates more like a Shakespearean aside. The content of language between these dashes is not necessarily subordinate to what goes before it, but elaborates and extends on the same level as the text of which it is a part.

Let's look to a few examples. Suppose you write, "Last year I saw my life on a sharp upward slope; everything was just great (or so I thought)." That is a fine use of parentheses, although that last phrase could have been set off as easily by a comma, with little loss in drama. What is within the parenthesis is subordinate, an afterthought to the main attraction. It would not be correct to have slung an em-dash after the word "great." But now consider this: "Last year I saw my life on a sharp upward slope—everything was surprisingly and unexpectedly great—until reality brought me back down to earth." This is a proper use of the em-dash, because the language in between the dashes works like an elaboration, or an aside, on the main subject. It would have been incorrect to stick that language inside parentheses.

Admittedly, it is not always easy to tell the difference between language that is subordinate and language that works like a Shakespearean aside. Typically, some pondering is necessary before deciding on the best choice, which suggests that these ornate forms of punctuation should be left to the more experienced writer. Learners have enough to master without worrying about the difference between parentheses and em-dashes. Certainly, when it comes to parenthetical statements and the use of em-dashes, less is definitely more—especially with em-dashes.

Quotations. Punctuation is a vast subject, much more so than most people realize. Quotation marks constitute a small subset of punctuation. The basic rules are simple and easy to find in any style guide, and so there is no reason to repeat that information here. I want only to comment on two minor matters, the first having to do with what happens when a writer wishes to leave out part of a quotation, because most of the time these days the proper way to do this is roundly ignored.

It is perfectly fine to leave out part of a quotation as long as by doing so one does not do violence to the original meaning of the text. The way one signals that something has been removed from the original is by use of what are called ellipses. There are two kinds of ellipses and they are typed differently in written work.

One kind, more common in fiction, is used when an author wishes to indicate that a voice is trailing off or that a thought is incomplete, as in: "Oh, I just can't take it anymore, my heart is all but broken and, well...." The other type of ellipses, used when one wishes to indicate that something has been removed from a quotation, looks like this: "We hold these truths to be self-evident, that all men are created equal, that they are endowed by their Creator with certain unalienable Rights, that among these are Life . . . and the pursuit of Happiness." As I have already indicated, these two different kinds of ellipses are typed differently, as any decent style guide will show you. In the "oral" ellipsis there are no spaces between the dots; in an "excerpt" ellipsis, there are.

Now, setting aside for the moment the fact that the removal of the word *liberty* borders on the philosophically and historically obscene, more sensitive than how to type ellipses is the question of where to put punctuation before and after quotation marks when they are part of an integral sentence. I am for the most part a law-abiding, rule-following sort of person, but I draw the line at the American way of doing these things. According to American usage, punctuation should go inside a close quotation mark, as in:

> The phrase "with liberty and justice for all," it is clear, is an ambition rather than a solid reality of American life.

You can see that the comma after the word "all" comes before the close quotation marks. That is how I have been doing it heretofore in this book, because I am writing it and the publisher is publishing it in the United States. But it makes absolutely no logical sense whatsoever. Inside the quotation marks there should be, and there should only be, what you are bringing to readers from others, from the past. If that comma, or question mark, or whatever it is does not abide in the original, then in my opinion it does not belong inside those quotation marks. "And I'll whip the man who says it isn't so," if you don't mind a lyric fragment from an old folk song and, yes, yet another comma placed where, by all that is right, true, and proper, it shouldn't be, but is.

British usage follows a more logical approach to punctuating quotations. When I worked for Owen Harries at *The National Interest*, who was of course trained in the British way, I discovered that he had created a hybrid arrangement, because the illogic of American usage in this regard bothered him at least as much as it bothers me. He fully adopted the British way except at the end of a sentence, where he allowed the period to go before the close quotation mark. (I am not sure why he made this exception.) In any event, I grew accustomed to this system and was content with it because it represented a major advance over the logic of the American way of doing such things. Then one day some years ago, when I was early in my tenure as editor of *The American Interest*, into my office came a man who turned out to be an even more extreme stickler about such things than I am. I will spare you the details of our conversation except to say that he practically dropped to his knees to beg me to adopt either the American or the British style fully, and to consign Mr. Harries's hybrid to the rubbish heap of stylesheets. I sympathized with his plaint, but I nonetheless threw him out of my office when, refusing to relent, he began quietly to sob.

If you are an American, or if you are conducting your professional life living and writing in America, then I advise you to use the American method in this respect of quotation punctuation, even as I am doing in this book. But I also advise you not to like it; indeed, I advise you not to like it at all.

Capitalization. If punctuation is to some extent a matter of taste and skill, the conventions of capitalization are as well. There are some words around which no ambiguity exists; in English, we either capitalize them or we don't. Proper names are capitalized, always. There is plenty of ambiguity left over to discuss, however.

As with punctuation, the conventions of capitalization have changed over time. It used to be, just 50 years ago, that standard proper English usage capitalized far more nouns than is the case today. The famous *Chicago Manual of Style* has led the charge toward lowercasing everything, or everything it could get its hands on, so it would seem. I dissent from this trend not merely as a matter of taste, but as a matter of efficiency and function.

At least one of the principal purposes of written language is to enable us to make distinctions. That's why, of course, having an extensive vocabulary is so important to good writing. The mindless lowercasing of nearly everything is so pernicious because it reduces our capacity to make distinctions in writing. It is almost equivalent to abolishing, say, 5 percent of our dictionary. Here are a few examples of what I mean.

We should wish to distinguish specific cases of a phenomenon from general descriptions of that phenomenon. So the Cold War describes a struggle between the United States and the Soviet Union that began a few years after World War II and ended more or less with the fall of the Berlin Wall in November 1989. That conflict was characterized at the same time by an intense ideological conflict and an enormous amount of mutual fear, but without an actual "hot" or shooting war ever breaking out directly between the two sides. (Incidentally, the term Cold War was a neologism invented by the famous American political commentator and critic Walter Lippmann. We will come to neologisms in a moment.) The same basic phenomenon has occurred at other times and in other places between other countries both before and especially after the onset of the U.S.–Soviet Cold War. For example, some scholars have referred to the competition during the 1950s and 1960s between Egypt under the rule of Gamal Abdel Nasser and Middle Eastern monarchies such as Saudi Arabia, Jordan, and Morocco as "the Arab cold war." Properly, they did not capitalize the term. Nowadays, however, most editors are instructed by the powers that be to lowercase references to the original Cold War. This, in my opinion, destroys our ability to distinguish between the specific original and the generic phenomenon of intense conflicts short of direct military hostilities. This is a step backward.

The same point applies to the word Western or West. We capitalize this word when it refers to a civilization—one, in this case, composed of three layers: the legacies in turn of classical Greece and Rome, Christendom, and the Enlightenment. We do not capitalize when it refers to a generic direction, as in, "If you want to get to Denver from St. Louis, you head west." It is therefore most unfortunate that editors often refuse to capitalize this word no matter how it is being used.

Many other examples could be put forth. It used to be that out of a sense of general respect the word President was always capitalized, as was the title Secretary of State, Secretary of Defense, and so forth, so long as it referred to actual officers of the American government. Again, to maximize our capacities to make distinctions, it made a certain amount of sense to lowercase these titles if one were referring not to a specific person holding the office, but rather to the generic role of that office within the architecture of American government. So if, for example, one wishes to say that "the secretary of state is nominated by the president but must be confirmed by the Senate," it makes a certain amount of sense to lowercase these titles. It doesn't make any sense when one is referring to specific persons who hold or have held these offices because, yet again, it diminishes our capacity to make distinctions.

Numbers and percentages. Different disciplines have different conventions for how writers are supposed to express numbers in written texts. You should adhere to the standard conventions of whatever discipline you are following. There are a few general rules, however, for writing outside academia, although there is no strong consensus on these rules.

The rule followed in this book is to spell out single-digit numbers, except for very large numbers such as 9 million people or $3 billion. For the magazines of which I have been editor, I have ruled that all percentages be expressed in numbers, not words. I also like to write out "percent" as one word rather than divide it into two or to use the "%" sign (except in graphs and charts). But this is a matter of taste. What is not a matter of taste is that, whichever convention you choose, you should use it consistently.

Finally on this point of writing about numbers, allow me to expostulate briefly on the alarming growth of decimal misuse. Decimals matter. Once a space shuttle launch had to be scrubbed when it was discovered that a calculation was an order of magnitude off because some dunce put a decimal in the wrong place. Far less consequential, but far more ubiquitous and infuriating, is the proliferation of decimals in writing about small quantities of money where they do not belong. One may refer to this problem as that of DMD proliferation—Decimals of Mass Destruction.

Not to insult the honorable doyens of your primary school education, but let's take care to be absolutely clear about this. If you want to write twenty-nine cents in mathematical symbols, you write either $0.29 or 29¢. The first term means twenty-nine one-hundredths of a dollar. You can tell that the number is twenty-nine one-hundredths because there is a decimal in front of the two and the nine. You can tell that we're talking about dollars because there is a dollar sign. Duh. The second term means twenty-nine cents. You can tell we're talking about cents because there is a cents sign. Again, duh. These mean the same thing because 100 cents make 1 dollar. Duh, duh, *duh*. But increasingly one sees, not only in handwritten signs in grocery stores and such, but also in printed and presumably proofread circulars, .29¢. This can only mean twenty-nine one-hundredths of a cent, which is a very small sum for anything these days when expressed as a price. Every once in a while, one will see $.29¢. As best I can make out, this can't possibly mean anything at all.

Folks, this is fifth-grade math at best, or at least it used to be. I am at a loss to explain why errant decimals are multiplying like cockroaches all over America. All I ask of you, dear reader, is that you not be part of the problem. If you want to become part of the solution, if you become incensed about this and decide to take vigilante action, I warn you that few merchants will appreciate your counsel in the constructive spirit with which you will no doubt offer it. Try it; you'll see.

"In fact," "exact same," "etc.," and other atrocities. As I have said on several occasions, some rules concerning writing style are technical and invariant, while others are merely matters of taste; however, the balance does shift around over time. For example, using *impact* as any kind of verb and using *grow* as a transitive verb, as in "to grow one's company," make my skin crawl, but these uses have become so common over the past 20 years that I realize full well the futility of complaining

about them; they have become by now mere matters of taste, whereas a few decades ago they were considered by the wizards of words to be plainly wrong.

There are many other locutions, too, that are neither one nor the other—neither wrong nor mere matters of taste. As a case in point, consider the short phrase *in fact* used at the beginning or in the middle of a sentence. Such use has become very common in recent times, and this is unfortunate. I try not to use the phrase *in fact* unless it exactly fits my meaning, which is a rare occasion. If you think about it, the phrase only works when a writer is trying to say that a discrete assertion which others claim is or is not literally true is actually the reverse of the claim. There is no other proper use of this phrase. Every other use should raise embarrassment, for if something is really true, then using *in fact* is redundant; if it isn't true, then using *in fact* qualifies as something between an error and a lie. It is therefore best avoided.

The increasingly common locution *exact same* is an even graver logical calamity. One tends to hear it more than one sees it in print, but one does occasionally see it in print, too—as for example in Tom Robbins's recent short novel *B Is for Beer*. It is utterly and obviously redundant: What can the word *exact* possibly add to the word *same,* or what can the word *same* possibly add to the word *exact?* Exactly nothing, that's what.

Now, it is not quite as bad to say or to write "exactly the same." At least in that case one would have an adverb doing what adverbs are supposed to do. I suppose, too, one could argue that "exactly the same" differs reasonably from "mostly the same" or "almost the same," but you would risk rebuttal from any philosophically literate person as to whether this really makes any sense either, given the dictionary meaning of the word *same.*

This mess with *exact same* falls into the category of trying to modify or conditionalize a word that does not easily take to modification by its very nature, like the word *pregnant* or the word *dead.* It is very hard to be half or partly pregnant, even though, arguably, a woman who is six months pregnant is "more" pregnant than a woman who is one month pregnant. And, except in figurative speech, it is hard to be half or partly dead. (Don't let things you may see very late on Saturday nights persuade you otherwise.)

The abbreviation *etc.* is also very popular in a whole range of writing disciplines. My advice to you is simple: Never use it. Whenever any serious intellect sees the abbreviation "etc." it has one meaning, and one meaning only. It means that the author knows that there is more to say or to list, but she either doesn't know what it is or is too lazy to be bothered finding out. Neither possibility makes for a good impression.

Finally in this group, let us interrogate the increasingly popular adjective *proactive*. Can anyone tell me what the *pro-* prefix to this word adds to *active*? Is *proactive* to be understood in contrast to *conactive,* which as far as anyone knows does not exist? What is wrong with the perfectly good word *active* all by itself? Nothing at all. *Proactive* is thus a bit like *exact same*—illogical because redundant, only in this case the redundancy is shoved into one word instead of two.

Again we return to a basic here: If you can't think straight—in this case think well enough to be able to recognize redundancy when it is staring you in the face—you can't write well. You should count on mistakes of this kind hurting you in the eyes of readers, even though, admittedly, these days an ever-fewer number of readers is liable to notice such things. Repeated grammatical oversights will hurt you (anyway) because they will cast a pall over your reputation, showering you with doubt by association as to whether you know what you are talking about even when you are not writing poorly.

Esoterica. I spilled much ink in Chapter 2 warning writers who wish to improve their skills to understand that less is more. Don't use many words when few will do as well. But that begs the question of which words to use. The answer depends on your purpose and especially on what your audience expects. In general, as I have already advised, don't use obscure words when common ones do just as well. Don't use long words when short ones are available.

There are exceptions to all rules, of course, including this one. In the midst of certain academic fields, one is expected to use disciplinary jargon, and there are many occasions when specialized language is capable of communicating among the initiated what ordinary language cannot. Specialized language can also be very economical. But the exception that I wish to convey to you is of a different nature.

Sometimes a certain word, though it is not widely known, is so perfect for the occasion that you simply must use it. There is no shame in driving people to the dictionary once in a while. I even do it deliberately in this book from time to time. But you should think of such occasions in the same way that you think of neologisms, edgy sounding subheads, and other high-risk literary tactics. Esoteric language will call attention to itself. Therefore, the risks of that distraction must not exceed the benefits. This is a judgment call, and to some extent a matter of taste. There are no hard-and-fast rules that can guide you here. Like everyone else, just do the best you can and let your experience guide you onward.

There is a special subcategory of esoteric language that warrants just a brief mention. Different languages are more or less diglossic. Now that is an esoteric, fancy word for you. What it means, simply put, is that some languages have very different spoken and written forms while others do not. Take Arabic and Hebrew, for example: Both are diglossic to a considerable extent. People write things they would never say and say things they would never write. American English, by contrast, is not very diglossic, but there are occasional examples. Thus, you see the word *eschew* in writing from time to time, but rarely hear anyone say it. You also see written the word *truculent,* but almost never hear anyone pronounce it correctly. You occasionally sees the word *niggardly* in writing; this word has absolutely nothing to do with racist slang by way of etymology, but many native English speakers think it does. You can use it if you want, but be prepared for the mindless frustrations that are likely to follow.

When in doubt, avoid these and similarly esoteric words. The reason is that, as we have already discussed, your job as a writer, all else equal, is to make life easy for your readers. Using words that cause readers to stumble doesn't do you any good. Sometimes it is a writer's task to challenge readers, and that certainly is not the same as making their lives easier. But the choice involves a trade-off, like a great many decisions in life. What makes no sense is annoying a reader and making her life difficult for no good reason. Don't let fancy words become your special fetish. They will not reward you well.

Neologisms. A neologism is a new word, something someone makes up because the language lacks a term suddenly thought to be necessary, or because the inventor is trying to draw special attention to a concept or idea. There is nothing wrong, and there can be much right, with using neologisms as long as you do not overdo it. But this, too, is a matter of taste. Some people like the wit inherent in neologisms, which usually involves twisting or joining together already existing vocabulary; others do not. Neologisms also work or fail depending on the sort of writing one is doing; a neologism, no matter how clever, just doesn't fit with a eulogy, for example. Their effective use depends ultimately on whether the cleverness in a particular neologism fits the subject and tone of the writing in which it is supposed to work.

Neologisms, because they are a form of wit, are subject to the same sensitivities and dangers as all other forms of wit in your writing. Humor translates poorly. Sarcasm translates never. Therefore, if you simply cannot resist inventing a word, be very careful to think it through before you use it.

Neologisms, however, when thought through and appropriate to the subject, can be of tremendous value. Sometimes a single word in the form of a neologism can constitute the title of an essay or even of a book. Sometimes, less grandly, a neologism works as a subhead within a larger piece of writing. The virtue of these literary inventions, when they work, is they have an almost supernatural capacity for condensation and economy in the expression of a concept. Sometimes, too, when a neologism is not crystal clear from the very start, but is merely suggestive, it has the benefit of stirring exactly the right amount of curiosity in potential readers. That, of course, is a very good thing.

You are doubtless seeking examples at this point, and as you have sought so you shall now find. There is the relatively new word *sheeple* to describe the oblivious, herdlike behavior of groups of people. There is the word *presstitute* to describe journalists who suck up uncritically to their sources. *Bullshistory* describes false, self-serving versions of the past. *Underdogma* describes the undeserved deference given to victims as a form of the current mode of political correctness. There is my creation of the term *Perhapsburg,* used as a title to an essay in my magazine, to suggest that the contemporary politics of the part of Europe that used to be within the Habsburg Empire might still be affected by that history. And then there is *Jewcentricity,* the title of one of my books, which is meant to entice readers into a discussion of exaggerations, both historical and contemporary, concerning Jews and Judaism.

Neologisms are high-stakes words. When they work, they work exceedingly well. But when they fail, they really go splat. The same goes for the use of slang, especially slang that borders on "dirty" language, and the same goes for alliteration, too. There are contexts in which slang and alliteration can work, again if you don't overdo them. But they are risky instruments. Any language that calls attention to itself risks distracting from the power of your writing at least as much as it has a potential to help it. Try your luck, or your skill, if you like, at neologisms, humor, slang, alliteration, and other gimmicks. Eventually, you will probably get the hang of it. Or not.

Before moving on to the next paragraph, I would be remiss not to point out that many aspects of language aside from gimmicks work fine when deployed sparingly or in moderation, but not when they are over-used or misused. Students often ask if it is possible to begin sentences with "and" or "but"; the answer is, yes, it's possible, and sometimes it's a good idea. As you can see, I do it myself, but in moderation, and so should you. Students also ask about the use of rhetorical questions. The answer is the same: They're fine, in their places. They're not fine in the wrong places, or in too many places.

Italics and boldface type. Finally in this regard, since we are talking about ways of emphasizing language, there is the question of how frequently to use italics and bold font in normal writing. At the risk of boring you, the answer is more or less the same: These gimmicks distract the reader by drawing attention disproportionately to the gim-mick. In political writing, the use of bold within prose is simply not done, so do not do it. Boldface type is restricted to titles and subheads, which are important enough to warrant such treatment. As for italics, it is appropriate to use them when referring to a word as a word, as I do in this book. It is a sign of poor writing, however, to overuse them, because it indicates that a writer is unable to produce emphasis by using his skills at composition. The best rule of thumb for the use of italics for *emphasis* is to use them only when there is inherent ambiguity as to where the would-be spoken emphasis is intended to be in a sentence. The crudest example I can think of appears above in this chapter. You will recall this sentence fragment: "Duh, duh, *duh*." Why italicize the third "duh"? Because I want to emphasize that I have stated an obvi-ous point for the third time running. Without the italics, this would be hard to do. The fragment might instead suggest toddler-speak at work, or something even less winsome.

Since word processors make it so easy to festoon writing with italics, boldface type, underlining, and Heaven-knows-what else, it's a good idea to check your work to make sure that you have not, in effect, turned your virtual moderator, inherent in your written voice, into a circus clown. The better a writer you become, the less need you will have for gimmicks of all sorts.

Oh, dear reader, are you to suppose now that, if you master all of the advice I have tendered in this chapter, you will then be a good, perhaps even an excellent, writer? Not on your life. After you have put 10,000 hours into the task, you will have earned the right to entertain such hopes. In the meantime, if you want to get better at writing, practice. Take the New Zealand-born short story writer Katherine Mansfield's experience to heart: In a 1922 journal entry, she wrote, "Looking back, I imagine I was always writing. Twaddle it was, too. But far better to write twaddle or anything, anything, rather than nothing at all."

All we have done in this chapter is to point out the most obvious delinquencies that afflict the inexperienced writer. We have searched for the torque points that, if studied and mastered, will give you enormous leverage and competitive edge over those still flailing about in the intellectual ether with no one to guide them, poor unfortunate souls that they are.

Having laid out these torque points and having provided guidance concerning them, we have created a basis to move on to the real subject of this little book: political writing, persuasive writing, writing to a purpose. Let us, then, now truly begin.

Recommended Reading

Lynne Truss, *Eats, Shoots & Leaves* (London: Profile Books, 2003).

Writing Exercise

Locate a fairly recent, relatively long piece of writing that you have composed—the longer the better in this case. Then go through it methodically, making a list of your transgressions of the 17 subsections of this chapter. Repair all cases of these transgressions and set your newly edited version next to the original.

Wait at least a full day, and then read the two versions—first the new, then the old—one right after the other. Next, take a clean piece of paper and a pen and write down just one word that best expresses your feelings on discerning the difference between the two versions. That word is the name of your journey up the mountain.

4 THE ESSAY[1]

When we talk of the polemical essay, we speak of a kind of writing that is very much specific to culture, to recall an important point from Chapter 1. Some cultures, and some periods within cultures, differ markedly from others in the way public discourse takes place. As it happens, most English-speaking countries have experienced, and still do, a very robust tradition of political contention in public and in various forms of literature: the essay, the pamphlet, the broadside, the newssheet, and others besides.

The English essay we know today as a secular expository piece of writing was more or less invented by the English statesman, scientist, and author Francis Bacon. The same form was invented in France at about the same time—actually a bit earlier—by the incomparable sixteenth-century writer Michel de Montaigne, but Bacon seems to have stumbled upon the idea independently. In any event, the essay blossomed forth in Britain in many forms, including essays fully grown into fanciful book-length allegories, from Jonathan Swift's *Gulliver's Travels* to George Orwell's *Animal Farm*. This tradition has also traveled to America, Canada, Australia, everywhere that Anglo-Saxons have gone—and that includes, with appropriate wrinkles accounted for, places as diverse as India, Jamaica, and Kenya.

Other cultures have similarly vibrant public political lives in literature, and of course France is a great and excellent example. But, for reasons not always clear, certain other political cultures never developed such strong forms of published polemic. Germany is a surprising example. Germans tend to either the technical or the philosophical in their writings. They have not excelled at the arts of policy polemic. Even today, my German colleague Josef Joffe complains of how boring German public life is compared to that in America, Britain, France, and even the Netherlands. Perhaps it has something to do with the

---

1. And the footnote.

character of German university life, where scholars tend not to involve themselves in public policy issues except in private consultation with government. They do not typically write op-eds, and compared to the huge array of policy magazines in the United States, there are few comparable publications in Germany.

Very much related, neither does Germany have anything like the think tank culture we have in America—but that is also true for the vast majority of countries. Think tanks perform an important function; they create the revolving door phenomenon. Now, many people think this is a bad thing. It's not, and here's why: It circulates mental air. A significant percentage of the polemical essays that make their way into American public policy debates are written by think tankers, or by those who have enjoyed associations with one or more such organizations over time.

Some think tanks are independent research organizations, some are adjuncts of universities, and some are connected to liberal or conservative ideological movements. The point is that think tanks, generally speaking, focus on issues of practical public policy concern. They do so far more than university research in the social sciences. The question is not one of bias; think tank studies and proposals are often biased, but then so are most of those generated by university faculty. No, the difference is that think tank senior staff are often either headed into or coming from government service. The experience of working in government tends to sharpen the focus toward practical matters in work done in both think tanks and universities, while the chance to concentrate on research in think tanks and universities benefits government when those researchers become policymakers. We mentioned Henry Kissinger earlier. He is a perfect example of the benefits of the revolving door. Dr. Kissinger brought to government from Harvard University a wealth of learning and insight, and he did so years before he became National Security Advisor and Secretary of State. From that experience he then brought back to Harvard invaluable knowledge of how government actually works. The same may be said for literally thousands of senior faculty in American universities, many thousands of think tank scholars and, not that it matters very much, for me. I, for example, could not explain to you in Chapter 7 what speechwriting in government is really like had I never done it myself.

I stress the point to emphasize the difference between the institutional matrix that embeds government, academia, and the nonprofit sector in general in the United States and the institutional matrix in practically every other country. I do this to teach that the nature of polemic in any given society is tied to key characteristics of its culture; so too, you will recall, is the nature of rhetoric. Both are and will remain expressions of larger social assumptions and trends.

Now, as it happens, in America the polemical political essay represents only a tiny fraction of the essays one may read in so very many places. In *Cosmopolitan*, for example, you can read essays about how to please, get, change, or dump your man. One might say that's more prurient than polemic. Indeed, in an age when virtually every area of human activity—from how to succeed in bocce ball to how to succeed in bed—has received saturation coverage, remarkably little attention has been given to the strategies and techniques of polemical debate. Just as there are so few courses in political science and government departments offered to teach you persuasive writing, there are few guides in writing to help you outside the classroom.

So, in a modest attempt to repair this omission, and in particular to help beginners avoid a long and tedious process of reinventing the wheel, I have some suggestions based on the trials and errors of my own experience, and also on the good counsel of others—including the aforementioned Owen Harries, whose genius is the original source of what follows. We together, then, offer you 12 rules for how to win arguments and influence debates.[2]

RULE 1: Forget about trying to convert your adversary as your principal objective. In any serious polemical confrontation (as opposed to genuine intellectual discourse), the chances of success on this score are so remote as to exclude it as a rational objective.

On the very rare occasions when it does happen, it will be because the person converted has already and independently come to harbor serious doubts concerning her existing position and is already teetering on the edge of defection. This will be due, more often than not, to some outrageous action by her own side or some shocking revelation: Witness the effect on members of Communist parties in the West of the Nazi-Soviet pact of 1939 and Nikita Khrushchev's 1956 speech denouncing Stalinism. Then, but only then, a particular argument or example in a

---

2. See Owen Harris's "Primer for Polemicists," *Tactical Notes* 10. Available at http://www.libertarian.co.uk/lapubs/tactn/tactn010.htm.

polemical essay may provide a catalyst to complete the process of ideo-logical conversion. An effective polemic can complete or seal a change of view, but almost never will it completely produce one.

Note, too, that when it comes to changing minds, the most effective avatars of change are former true believers in a position since abandoned. When prominent individuals publicly change their views on fundamen-tal questions, they often bring in tow many less prominent individuals with them. Most of the time in recent decades, in Western societies at least, the direction has been from left to right. It mattered (whether for better or for worse is not the point), when the extraordinarily skilled polemicist Christopher Hitchens (1949–2011) abandoned his column at the very left of center magazine *The Nation* and became an energized advocate for the Bush administration's war in Iraq. As an intermediate agent of change, Hitchens writing as a defector from the left was a far more consequential event than anything that might have been written by someone who had never been on the left in the first place. In his journey, Hitchens followed many earlier apostates from revolutionary socialism, including the six brought together in the famous 1949 book *The God That Failed.* In accordance with the maxim that it takes one to know one, ideological movements should go out of their way to feature such apostates in their propaganda efforts if they can.

If persuading one's opponents is not the principal objective of a polemical essay, then what is or should be one's principal objective? Patience, please; I will get to that in a moment.

RULE 2: Pay great attention to the agenda of the debate. He who defines the issues and determines their priority is already well on the way to winning. That is why, to take a recent example, there was such a determined attempt just after September 11, 2001, to contest the initial definition of the issue: Was the debate about terrorism and terrorists, or was it about American arrogance, made-in-the-USA globalization, or some other alleged transgression centered in Washington, DC, or on Wall Street?

It is essential in this regard to resist semantic aggression, which is to say, to prevent your opponents from imposing their language and concepts on the debate. Always use terms that reflect your own prin-ciples, traditions, and interests. Never absentmindedly give in to the choices of others whose predilections do not match your own. Consider the use of loaded terms like racism and genocide: These words connote the very opposite of mom and apple pie in the American context. They have the effect, when they stick on a subject, of totally sterilizing the possibility of useful debate. So if what was going on in the Balkans, and especially in Bosnia-Herzegovina, in the mid-1990s was really genocide, then any argument against the use American military force to stop it was bound to sound like hard-hearted, unreasonable moral illiteracy. But if it was not genocide, then one could have a reasonable discussion about American interests, capabilities, and options short of military intervention.

Rather the same thing was at play in the decision of the Obama administration in mid-March 2011 to intervene militarily in Libya. If one believed that an impending regime attack on the city of Benghazi amounted to imminent genocide, it became far more difficult to argue prudentially against intervention. If, instead, one believed that the possibility of genocide in Benghazi amounted to a counterfactual of unknowable provenance, then that would open an altogether different kind of discussion.

Sometimes the battle for vocabulary does not turn over particular episodes, but abides in broader and deeper themes that are essentially ideological in nature. The selective and asymmetrical use of labels like *conservative* and *right-wing* constitute a good example. All newspapers exhibit some kind of general bias, and it borders on ridiculous to complain about that bias. If you don't like a newspaper's bias, don't read it; read something else instead. That seems simple enough. The *New York Times*, for example, being these days on most domestic social issues somewhat left of center, is apt to apply the label *right-wing* when *conservative* would be just as accurate, if not more so, any time the editors disapprove of what is being labeled. Readers of the *Times* are highly unlikely to see *liberals* or *progressives* referred to as *socialists* or *left-wingers* by the paper's editorial staff. Of course, as is to be expected, you will find precisely the reverse tendencies at a right-of-center publication like the weekly *National Review*.

Carelessness or misplaced tolerance in respect to foundational vocabulary can be enormously costly to any polemicist. You must insist on your choice of vocabulary, and you would be within your rights to explicitly attempt to "out" the biased vocabulary of your opponents. That is fair game, and it is a game much to your advantage if you have confidence that you can get the goods on the bad guys—that is, those who oppose your view.

RULE 3: Preaching to the converted, far from being a superfluous activity, is vital. Preachers do it every Sunday. The strengthening of the commitment, intellectual efficacy, and morale of those already on your side is an essential task, both in order to bind them more securely to the cause and to make them more persuasive exponents of it.

As shown by religious movements in earlier times and the anti-Vietnam war and civil rights movements more recently, conviction and dedication are enormous assets, often more than compensating for lack of numbers. On the negative side, one of the most embarrassing experiences in a polemical exchange is to have one's own case misrepresented and mangled by one's own allies. One can try to be clear but, alas, idiots will be idiots and there's not much anyone can do about it. Well, there is one thing you can do about it: Make sure you're not the idiot.

RULE 4: Never forget the uncommitted: Almost invariably, they constitute the vast majority, and here, as promised, is your true principal objective as a polemicist.

This may seem obvious on reflection, but in the excitement of combat and lust for the polemical "kill," the uncommitted are often overlooked, trampled, as it were, in the heat of battle. The polemical encounter becomes an end in itself rather than a means of influencing wider opinion. Yet understand well that what works best in throwing opponents off balance—cleverness, originality, pugnacity, ridicule—is often counterproductive with the neutral or undecided, who are more likely to be impressed by good sense, decency, and fairness.

Attentive readers will recognize here an example of what we learned in Chapter 2 to call the multiple-audience problem. One must know one's purpose, and one must know one's main audience before one can write effectively, but, as already pointed out, limiting one's audience is not so easy to accomplish. One must exercise acute situational awareness in order to avoid alienating the uncommitted, even sometimes at the expense of disappointing one's fellow true believers.

RULE 5: Once aware, as if by second nature, that you may have a multiple-audience problem, you must decide your course based on your purpose. There is no hard-and-fast rule for deciding which tact to take, but your purpose should always be your guide.

This wise counsel came to me by way of a particularly memorable experience. The first time I went in to see Secretary of State Powell to get his guidance for a particular major speech, I asked him, "OK, sir, what do you want to say?" As I asked him this question, I sat with my pen ready for action, my notebook on my lap. He did not answer.

Instead he fixed me eyeball to eyeball, and then slowly shook his head in dramatically intended disappointment. After a moment or two, he answered: "No, no, no, Adam. Never ask me what I want to say. Ask me what I want *to do*. Ask me what I want to achieve with this speech, or any speech. I hired *you* to figure out how to say it."

The proverbial lightbulb ignited in my head. I got it. I had learned a very important lesson. Purpose comes first, audience comes second, and the words follow.

Now, you will not always have some boss like Colin Powell, or any boss at all, to tell you your purpose. Sometimes you will have to figure it out on your own. Like so much else in life, this type of prudential judgment is cultivated over a lifetime. Central to any such decision is a trade-off, and in any trade-off one becomes sensitive to both the need for and the occasional costs of compromise and restraint. You might choose to make a sharply focused pitch to a particular audience, even at the risk of alienating others. Or you might choose to strike some sort of balance between the two, which is always more appealing than it turns out easy to do. But whatever you choose, the important thing is to choose a course and stick with it.

Again, why belabor what seems such an obvious point? Because for all I know, you might get yourself mixed up with a bunch of intellectuals. Politicians readily understand the need to choose an audience. They are usually unperturbed about having to sacrifice impact on a limited group for breadth of appeal. This is one reason their utterances so often appear anodyne and bland. On the other hand, intellectuals—who tend to regard all who are not intellectuals as unimportant, and who tend to equate compromise with sin—are particularly inept in this respect, which is why their victories are so often Pyrrhic in character. They may "win" an argument or a debate, but leave such a bad taste in people's mouths that they end up having won little indeed. It is a phenomenon reminiscent of a remark about war and peace once made by the great twentieth-century French thinker Raymond Aron: "There are ways of conquering that can transform victory into defeat." Now there is a candidate for your young quotations file!

RULE 6: Be prepared to go around the block many times. When you have a good point to make, keep making it. Success in ideological polemics is very much a matter of staying power and indomitable will.

Communists used to understand this rule very well and practiced it to excess. In a much less consequential setting, Communists proved their aptitude at this when they encountered the firebrands of the New Left on American university campuses in the late 1960s and early 1970s. The avatars of the New Left, their insistence on authenticity on their lips and their bong in their hands, were no match for Communist "straights" who were prepared to stay at meetings designed to hammer out common positions on antiwar strategy until all of their hip colleagues had wandered off or fallen asleep in their chairs. Guess who, despite their being a distinct minority, got to decide the agenda much of the time?

Western politicians vary in respect to their capability for repetition. When he served as British Prime Minister, Tony Blair was always "on message"; President George W. Bush was not afraid of being repetitious either. They both understood how political controversies play out. But intellectuals, who put a high professional premium on novelty and originality and often possess a great fear of being thought boring by their peers, have greater difficulties. In my opinion, as a former speechwriter for two Republican Secretaries of State, President Obama in some respects illustrates this fear. He has been unusually reticent as a national leader in times of great strain. Sometimes it seems as if he has simply disappeared from the scene, his voice gone missing from the debate. Perhaps he assumes that once he gives a speech, everyone should understand what he said, so that there is no need for him to say it again. One reason for this may be that he is too much an intellectual to feel comfortable saying the same thing over and over again, even though that is sometimes what it takes in politics to win your way.

Those of this disposition might consider pinning on their study walls a passage from Saul Bellow's book, *Mr. Sammler's Planet*:

> It is sometimes necessary to repeat what all know. All mapmakers should place the Mississippi in the same location and avoid originality. It may be boring, but one has to know where it is. We cannot have the Mississippi flowing toward the Rockies, just for a change.

You might also put it up alongside Lord Wellington's remark at Waterloo: "Hard pounding this, gentlemen; let's see who will pound longest."

RULE 7: Shave with Occam's razor.[3] Knowing what you can afford to give away is one of the great arts of polemic. It is truly astonishing,

---

3. If you still do not know what is meant by Occam's razor, despite its prior appearance at the bottom of page 36, find out.

but even experienced polemicists often expend an absurd amount of time and energy defending what is irrelevant or peripheral to their case. Thus, if one wishes to defend the proposition that the United States is the freest and most creative country in the world, there is no need to deny that it is also a violent society, any more than it was once necessary to contest that Adolf Hitler built good roads or that Benito Mussolini made the trains run on time in order to establish their evilness. Practicing polemical economy narrows the area you have to defend, and it gives you more time or space, as the case may be, to concentrate on what is really essential to your position.

RULE 8: Be very careful in your use of examples, especially historical analogies. As often as not, their illustrative value is outweighed by their distracting effect. People will tend to concentrate on the factual content of the particular episode to which you are referring, the validity of your account, or the legitimacy of analogies in general, and ignore the original point you were trying to make. Thus, for example, any references to the appeasement policies of the 1930s in the context of a discussion, say, of American policy toward China today, is likely to bring progress to an end and precipitate a prolonged wrangle over the precise circumstances of the occupation of the Rhineland or the writings of Winston Churchill. This will not prove a useful diversion.

Yes, of course, analogies are often a powerful and persuasive way of bringing a point home. But you should generally be economical in their use, careful in their choice, and well armed to defend the ones you do choose. You should realize, too, upon a moment's reflection, that the insight insisting "hindsight is 20/20" is just another one of those common, comforting lies we hear but never think to interrogate. If hindsight were 20/20, then the task of writing archival history well would be no serious challenge. It most certainly is, however, as anyone who has ever tried to do it knows.

RULE 9: Avoid trading in motives as an alternative to rebutting the opposing case. Or, in the words of the American philosopher Sidney Hook, "Before impugning an opponent's motives, even when they may legitimately be impugned, answer his arguments."

This laudable admonition is routinely ignored by many opinion journalists and intellectuals. Indeed, many often attribute and attack motives as the first step in a debate. Witness the way that much-needed public discussion of racial inequality in America, and of social justice generally, is inhibited and poisoned by the charges of racism readily leveled against anyone critical of the liberal orthodoxy on these issues. Once again, we are reminded of the critical importance of controlling the vocabulary of debate.

Sidney Hook's advice is worth following for two reasons: First, it is the proper thing to do and you will feel better for doing it. Second and more important, motives are irrelevant to the soundness of an argument. Anything that is said by someone whose motives are suspect could equally well (and in all probability will) be uttered by someone whose motives are impeccable, and an answer will still be required. Motives can explain error, distortion, and falsehood in an argument, but they cannot establish the truth or falsity of the argument itself. That, as they say in philosophical circles, is a category error.

The place to discuss motives, if you feel compelled to discuss them at all, is not at the beginning but at the end of an essay, when the facts have been established and the errors of your opponents have already been exposed for what they are. You will usually find, however, that if you have done all of this well, your eagerness to delve into matters of motive will have dissipated. That is as it should be.

RULE 10: Emulate the iceberg. In any polemical exchange, whether in writing or in oral form, make sure that you know several times more about a topic than you can conceivably use or show in speech or writing. This is important, for one thing, because you will not know in advance what precisely you will have to use on any given occasion of speaking or even of writing. Even more important, the fact that you have much in reserve (which will usually become evident through an accumulation of small touches) will give a resonance and authority to what you do use.

By way of example, note the difference between the writing of the genuinely knowledgeable and the instant experts on anything Middle Eastern and Islamic in recent years. After the 9/11 attacks, demand exceeded supply by several orders of magnitude. As a predictable result, hordes of hungry journalists vied to satisfy that demand. But recalling the 10,000-hour rule, it is not possible to become truly expert on such subjects in just a few days or even a few months. Most of these purveyors of instant wisdom instead purveyed a great deal of misunderstanding and flat error. I cannot resist one example.

I wish I had a nickel for every time some instant expert told an audience that whereas Christianity historically separated church and

state, Islam did not. This is a very popular vulgarism that confuses
theory with history because those who mouth or write it clearly know
very little history. For most of the period between the year 313, when
Constantine made Christianity the state religion of the Roman Empire,
and 1517, when Martin Luther nailed his famous paper to the church
door in Wittenberg, the Catholic Church disposed of very considerable
military power. The clergy of Islam, having no ecclesiastical hierarchy
comparable to that of the Catholic Church, and divided into many
states from Morocco to India and beyond, never exercised temporal
authority except during the first 90 years of Islamic history. Anyone
who knew even just this much history, let alone those who actually
knew the subject well, could vivisect a fake instant expert in a matter
of seconds, slicing him from "dimple to duodenum," as Don Marquis
once put it via his unforgettable character Mehitabel the Cat.[4]

But, alas, true experts on the region and its culture, largely ensconced
in elite universities of various descriptions, lacked the theatrical panache
of journalists and were particularly poorly practiced in the art of the
electronic media's sound bite. They tended by default to propel themselves into 40-minute lecture mode, which does not amuse someone
holding a microphone up to their face. They were excellent icebergs,
but few ever made it to the show.

RULE 11: Know your opposition. Always bear in mind John Stuart
Mill's observation that he who knows only his own position knows little
of that. Understand the position of your adversary not in a caricatured
or superficial form but at its strongest, for until you have rebutted it
at its strongest you have not rebutted it at all.

This is a necessary condition both for developing your own position
fully and for attacking your opponent successfully. It was no accident, as
we have already noted, that many of the most effective anti-Communists
were those who at one stage of their lives had been either in or very
close to a Communist Party.

RULE 12: Before employing these or any other debating stratagems,
make every effort to ensure that the position you decide to defend is

---

4. Looking for good fiction? You could do a lot worse than Marquis's *Archy and
Mehitabel*, first published in 1927.

intellectually, morally, and politically worthy of your efforts, and especially that you actually have something worth saying. Being on the side of the good and the true and the right does not guarantee success, but, other things being equal, it helps.

Essays can be extremely powerful vehicles of persuasion. Not only can they convince readers, especially the minions of the uncommitted and still open-minded, on discrete policy issues, they can frame entire subjects in a way that predisposes a generation of thought about them. George Kennan's 1947 *Foreign Affairs* essay, "The Sources of Soviet Conduct," signed by "X," is perhaps the best example from recent decades. This essay created and canonized the concept of containment, which remained the intellectual anchor of U.S. foreign policy throughout more than a half century of Cold War. Francis Fukuyama's 1989 essay in *The National Interest*, "The End of History?" very nearly did the same. Very influential essays such as these do not always break new substantive ground; sometimes they succeed by articulating sensibilities already thick in the air, and especially by integrating into a unitary framework an otherwise unorganized mass of conceptual fragments.

Such essays do not come along very often, but one feature they all have in common is that they are skillfully written. Having a great idea is a necessary element of a powerful essay, but not a sufficient one. To be truly powerful, the writing must be worthy of the thinking.

Unfortunately, it is very difficult to come up with specific rules for writing polemical essays, since topics vary so much and the audience you choose will dictate the tone you take. If you are seeking to morally arm your allies, you will choose pulse-raising language you would wisely avoid were your audience composed mainly of fence-sitters. But aside from that, there are only two points worth emphasizing above and beyond the strictures of good writing in general that apply to all polemical essays.

The first of these concerns balance. Once you know your purpose and your audience, and have crafted your logic and vocabulary to win the day, you must focus your energies—again, iceberg-like—on those assets and aims. You must not write a dozen sentences on some side or supporting point while spending only two or three on the main show. Writers get unbalanced for one of two reasons most of the time: They're trying to show off how much they know, or they're thinking on paper, wrestling with some intriguing material they've yet to fully comprehend. If the former, an ego leash is called for, and if the latter, a bit more patience would help.

The second general point is this: Don't bury your "lede"—as journalists spell it for some strange reason. They mean "lead," which otherwise translates as thesis or main point. In English-language polemics, the custom and therefore the reader's expectation is that the essayist will hit him with the main point of all these words up front. So you should do that. You do not need to do it in full frontal mode all the time, for it is often shrewd writing to foreshadow, or "show a little leg" early on, only to reserve the real knockout punch for a strategic point later on. What you can't do, or at any rate shouldn't do, is ramble on for introductory page after page without focusing the reader's attention on your point, and hence your purpose.

Your own stern editing can correct this problem. Many writers need buckets of ink for purposes of throat clearing before they can summon the clarity of mind to actually say anything interesting or useful. That's fine, as long as such writers go back and get rid of all that verbal phlegm before they finish the job. You as an author with a purpose need to know your thesis expressed in succinct and powerful language. If after you think you have finished drafting an essay you review your text and can find no such thesis anywhere in sight on your first page or two, you are not finished—because you need to find and reposition your "lede."

Now, for the footnote or, in degraded form, the endnote. There is a fine book by Anthony Grafton that gives you the history of the footnote as an ancillary literary form, at least as far as historians are concerned.[5] There is another, more recent, by Chuck Zerby called *Devil's Details: A History of Footnotes.*[6] Both show how the footnote has changed form and purpose over time, which is consistent with the observation that all aspects of language are embedded in larger cultural flows. What neither does do, except cursorily, is tell you how these devices get used today in polemical exchanges. That is the purpose of the final section of this chapter.

You will not be surprised to learn, I hope, that writers of political polemic do not generally wish to tell their prospective readers that they are engaged in polemic. *Polemic* is not a dirty word, but it certainly is not as respectable a word as *analysis,* let alone *scholarship.* Those with particular

---

5. Anthony Grafton, *The Footnote: A Curious History* (Cambridge, MA: Harvard University Press, 1997).

6. Chuck Zerby, *Devil's Details: A History of Footnotes* (New York: Touchstone, 2003).

points of view trying to achieve certain political goals generally guard their aims by wrapping them in a patina of respectability. Footnotes featuring respected sources advance this aim because they lend legitimacy to arguments whose premises might otherwise lay naked to view.

Many magazines in the policy world, magazines that think tank researchers as well as academics publish in on a regular basis, do not particularly like footnotes and tend to discourage them. Indeed, many people have had nasty things to say about footnotes over the years. They have been called "unsightly," "forbidding," "like a fungus," even an "excrescence." According to Alexandra Horowitz, Noël Coward reputedly said that "having to read a footnote resembles having to go downstairs to answer the door while in the midst of making love."[7] Any publication that lacks footnotes is thereby distinguished from a journal, especially a journal that is juried in the proper scholarly fashion, where footnotes are obligatory and numerous. And there are other publications, like my own, *The American Interest*, which lies somewhere between a magazine and a journal. We allow and even encourage footnotes when they are essential for establishing a logical direction and a paper trail, and especially if they relieve an author of having to detail such matters in the text; but we discourage the decorative footnotes that festoon academic work in profusion.

While we're at it, let us also take note of the difference between a footnote and an endnote, insofar as there is any difference, and there isn't much of one. A footnote appears at the foot of the page, naturally enough. An endnote is the same text but appears at the end of an essay, chapter, or book. For some combination of marketing and technical reasons, endnotes became more popular than footnotes for a time. On occasion, both appeared in the same publication, the footnote containing any discursive content and the endnote being a mere source. All of this was and remains unfortunate for the simple reason that the more effort a reader has to put forth to find a note, the less likely she will bother. To the extent notes go unread because of their placement, it just defeats the purpose of their existence in the first place.

Clearly, to return to our main line of argument, legitimacy rests in the eye of the beholder, which means, in this case, the reader. Sometimes a footnote will refer to a source that is above controversy or

---

7. Alexandra Horowitz, "Will the E-Book Kill the Footnote?" *New York Times Book Review*, October 9, 2011.

reproach—to a venerable classic of universal appeal. But sometimes in the world of policy debate a footnote is meant to indicate which school of thought the writer respects and follows. For others in the same school of thought, such footnotes function as a means of reassurance. They tell the reader, in so many words, that this author is trustworthy. She has good pedigree, or the proper intellectual breeding, so to speak. In many ways, footnoting for the purpose of ideological reassurance resembles a kind of intellectual apostolic succession. Obviously, for those of other schools, to one degree or another, this kind of footnoting can raise danger signals, as if to say, this fellow is not of our persuasion, and so is to be presumed guilty until proven innocent. In short, a footnote can carry with it either guilt or vindication by association.

A writer is wise to know the signals that footnotes send to various groups of readers. This is another way of saying that a writer must know his purpose and his audience. If you are writing in a quixotic effort to persuade your opponents of your own point of view, then cite footnote sources they respect, albeit sometimes in ways they do not expect. You would be unwise to footnote sources that will automatically raise their repugnance. If, on the other hand, you are writing to those already of your school, your footnote strategy would be different.

To give you just a few simple examples, anyone who quotes the Russian American philosopher and novelist Ayn Rand (first name rhymes with "mine") favorably immediately signals, among other things, a libertarian inclination and, probably, a deep hatred of meliorist liberals in general and of Woodrow Wilson in particular. Anyone who quotes the Austrian economists Ludwig von Mises or Friedrich Hayek favorably also signals a libertarian inclination, but a milder one carrying no specific attitude toward the late President Wilson. Anyone who quotes Noam Chomsky, a self-described libertarian socialist, favorably—at least in writings where Chomsky is not limiting himself to linguistics—signals to readers that he is a member of the adversary culture, decidedly outside of the contemporary mainstream debate. The more experience one has in any field of public policy analysis and debate, the more knowledgeable one becomes about the signaling power of references to others. This does not go on only in footnotes, but it does go on very much in footnotes.

Part of the legitimacy endowed on a piece of writing by footnotes is the intimation that the writer is following the professional canon, that he has observed the rules of logic and evidence serious people expect of reliable analysis. It is therefore important to write footnotes correctly, or the impression will soon turn to a wasting asset. There are several systems for writing footnotes. They tend to vary depending on the discipline. If you look in any style manual, you will see how these things are done. In this book, the few footnotes I use follow standard *Chicago Manual of Style* form, or the more scholarly guide distilled from that school of style known universally as *Turabian,* after its original author, Kate Turabian. It is the most logical of all the choices open to you. But again, if your discipline requires another form, that is fine. The key is to be consistent.

Footnotes have many functions beyond the legitimacy they lend to the argument of a polemicist. One of these concerns economy, and it elides on the multiple-audience problem. If you take seriously the advice that less is more, then you will understand that in an essay you will not wish to use more words than necessary to convey your meaning. On the other hand, you will not wish to make your prose so dense and minimalistic that many readers will fail to understand you. Footnotes can help you bridge this problem. It is sometimes helpful to think of your text as your argument, and your footnotes as your proof—or at least a guide to your proof. This does not mean that you should abandon all hopes of logical flow in your writing; it simply means that you can lend authority to your argument below the line in the way you reference other materials relevant to your subject matter.

Beyond simple references, you may also write discursive footnotes, in which you add comments to your text in order to clarify your meaning for those readers who may not grasp it. For example, you may use a particular term of the art that clued-in readers understand but some others may not. Rather than clutter your text with definitional matters, it is perfectly acceptable to drop the definition into a footnote, and then to reference the source of the definition.

Even that is not all. I have warned you to take care against blithely assuming that readers will readily understand your uses of humor, sarcasm, and irony. But if you simply cannot help yourself, you have the option of dropping these literary bombs into footnotes rather than keeping them in your text. This used to be a particularly popular method several decades ago, and sophisticated writers still do it from time to time. The use of footnotes in this fashion also accomplishes another task: It helps keep your tone even. It is not a good thing to bounce around from the serious to the blithe in your writing, so footnotes—because they mark a departure from your primary text—can be used to add an emotional emphasis without disrupting the main flow of your prose. In the same vein, personal reflections that are inappropriate in tone for the text can sometimes work if they are relegated to footnotes.

Some writers are tempted to use footnotes to introduce parallel discussions of the subject on hand that might deflect from attention were they in the main text. Generally, this is not a good idea for polemical writing, because any distraction from the point or points you are trying to make diminishes the power of your presentation. The broad rule here is that if language is not important enough to be in the main text, then it is not important enough to be in a footnote at any length. In scholarly work, or work that is somewhat less than purely polemical, this sort of diversion is less risky. Again we are confronted with a matter of taste; some people enjoy the multilevel discussion that discursive footnotes allow, and some do not. And, as you know, there is no accounting for taste.

There are two further manifestations of footnotes you should be aware of, although I doubt you will have recourse to use them yourself. One of these is called the Washington footnote.

The Washington footnote is created not by anything a writer does, but by something a reader does. Well-known people in Washington who inhabit the political circuits are often quite sensitive to their public image. So when a book appears written by an insider, or by a journalist like Bob Woodward who has access to insiders, these well-known people will scour the index looking for references to themselves. If they find any, they will immediately turn to the pages referenced to see what the author has to say about them and about their closest associates. Much of the time such references will be found in footnotes, for another use of footnotes is to relegate ad hominem comment to them. If they do not find any, they will be either sad or relieved, depending on the circumstances, defined by who the author is and what targets of opportunity he is aiming to hit.

The second special, rather exotic use of footnotes concerns spoofs or takeoffs. Footnotes are, to most people, indicators of egg-headed activity of one kind or another. Americans think of themselves as pragmatic people and their attitude toward some intellectuals is, at times quite justifiably, suspicious. They are particularly ready to lampoon those spouting indecipherable jargon but who, at the same time, cannot seem to tie their shoelaces properly or dress themselves without evoking gales of laughter. Some writers of humorous prose have therefore latched onto the footnote as a device for poking fun.

You can find examples in many places, but the most entertaining one I can recommend is a book by James Thurber and E.B. White, published in 1929, called *Is Sex Necessary? Or, Why You Feel the Way You Do*. As you may know, James Thurber was one of America's greatest writers, and E.B. White, the author of *Charlotte's Web* and a full principal in the *Strunk & White* style guide, was no slouch either. This book is a spoof of the then new genre of sexual self-help books, and some of its funniest lines reside in footnotes.

Speaking of funny, let us conclude this chapter on essays by observing that political life, as contentious as it can be, is not without its entertainment value. People who work in this world may have very serious ambitions and callings, but they are still human beings who appreciate to one extent or another the foibles of the human condition. A good essayist, which is not much different from saying an effective essayist, must learn to use tone to his advantage. You must know when to be serious and when to lift the veil just a bit to make room for, if not humor, then wit. It is a dirty little secret of effective polemic, one that I am now unveiling for you, that persuasion and entertainment are two sides of the same persuasive sword. If your mastery of style and tone can of themselves be pleasing to readers, whether in your text or in your judicious use of footnotes, you are way ahead in your effort to get them to buy into your argument.[8] If your style is awkward and your tone hectoring, you will turn readers off before they even have an opportunity to become ensnared by your logic. Above all, perhaps, the worst sin in polemical writing is to be inappropriately lacking of wit.

These days, fewer and fewer young people can tell the difference

---

8. Here is an example for you of a parallel discussion in a footnote that may hold interest, and that is of a personal nature, but that down here below the line won't interfere with the flow of the prose. I was once briefly an encyclopedia salesman, of the door-to-door type. I did this in the summer after my graduation from high school, and before I went to the University of Pennsylvania in the fall. I did not sell many encyclopedias. If memory serves me, I sold exactly one more set than the number of dogs who bit me in the leg. But that is not important. What is important here is that we salesmen were trained by experts in how to "get in the door," because if you don't get in the door to pitch your product, you'll never sell it. The way you get in the door is as follows: When someone opens the door you greet (usually) her smilingly, tell her you are doing some work in the neighborhood, and then ask, as you very deliberately lock eyes and nod your head up and down, if you might come in to show and talk about your wares. You keep looking at her directly in the eye as you subtly nod your head up and down because the answer you are seeking to your question is "yes." What we learned—since we had never thought about it before—is that when you look somebody in the eye and begin moderately to nod your head up and down, they begin to nod their head up and down too, and it is very difficult for someone who is nodding her head up and down to say "no" (unless she is Bulgarian, but that is not something I want to explain right now).

between paradox and irony, and few have ever been asked to think about the difference between humor and wit. Perhaps the best way to distinguish humor from wit is to observe that humor makes us laugh without, but that wit makes us laugh within. When a writer makes a reader laugh within, he has established an instantaneous community of intimacy with that reader. Little is more effective at persuasion than the creation of such communities. This is an observation that runs parallel to one by the Irish-born poet W.B. Yeats, who observed that we make rhetoric out of quarrels with others, but poetry out of quarrels with ourselves.[9] (Your quotation file is growing by the minute, isn't it?) When your efforts at rhetoric turn into poetry in the hearts and minds of your readers, that's when you've made it, and made it big.

---

9. Paraphrased from Yeats's essay "Anima Hominis," in *Per amica silentia lunae* (New York: Macmillan, 1918).

Recommended Reading

Francis Bacon, *Of Boldness* (Whitefish, MT: Kessinger Publishing, 2006).

Francis Fukuyama, "The End of History?" *The National Interest*, Summer 1989.

Colin L. Powell, "A Strategy of Partnerships," *Foreign Affairs*, January/February 2004.

David H. Petraeus & Ralph Peters, "To Ph.D. or Not to Ph.D.?—That Is the Question," *The American Interest*, July/August 2007.

Anthony Grafton, *The Footnote: A Curious History* (Cambridge, MA: Harvard University Press, 1999), ch. 1.

Writing Exercise

Analyze together the Petraeus and Peters essays in terms of their persuasiveness. Your essay should be between 500 and 1,000 words in length, and *it* should be as persuasive as you can make it.

5 THE REVIEW

The review essay is a little like the footnote in the sense that all sorts of skullduggery and cleverness may reside there. And it is a little like a polemical essay in that it means to persuade its reader. Also, as with essays, reviews come in many forms: persuasion about policy issues; persuasion about ideological templates; persuasion about cultural issues; even persuasion about tastes. The difference is that the occasion of the publication of a book, or books, or the holding of an art exhibit and so on, is the platform upon which the arts of persuasion play out.

This difference automatically creates sparks that ordinary essays cannot: The publication of a book, or books, represents in itself much of the time an attempt to persuade. So a review, then, is an attempt to persuade based on an attempt to persuade. It is a triangle of persuasion involving the author of the book or books under review, the writer of the review, and the reader. If the reader of the review has already read the items being reviewed—a rare but not unheard of state of affairs—then the reader is at least potentially in a position to judge the reviewer. Now this amounts to a turning of the tables that does not happen in the usual play of writing and reading ordinary polemical essays. This shows that a review essay bears a unique geometry among the art forms of literary persuasion.

Before pursuing this observation, we need to make two detours, one small and one not quite so small.

First, books are not the only productions of culture that get reviewed these days. Films have been the subject of reviews for decades, and stage plays have been reviewed for centuries. Even video games get reviewed, and such reviews can have surprising political content. There is a not entirely unserious argument over whether, say, playing any of the various iterations of *Grand Theft Auto* is a suitable thing for 11-year-olds to be doing. Restaurants get reviewed. Art and architecture get reviewed—both shows and individual buildings, and people who do them. In *The American Interest,* I have even run reviews of new pinball machines, tattoos, and chic international high mucky-muck meetings like those held annually in Davos, Switzerland, for the World Economic Forum.

Note that the so-called dark arts of persuasion enter into all of this, even if it is persuasion about aesthetic matters rather than overtly political ones. But remember, both politics and aesthetics fit into the framework of philosophy, and recall that philosophy is, in its essence, human reflection on human nature: the power of consciousness reflecting on consciousness itself and its creations. So these subjects are not so dissimilar as some might think.

Second, you have no doubt heard of the term *critic*. What is a critic, and what is the connection between someone who reviews books and other cultural artifacts and someone who critiques them? There is no unambiguous answer to this question; it's a matter of degree, but not a trivial matter of degree. A reviewer is someone who reviews, but who also does other things, and *mainly* other things, such as teach, or work in government, or whatever. A critic is someone whose main activity is passing judgment on and interpreting the works of others. So all critics are reviewers, but not all reviewers are critics.

But what does it really mean to be an effective critic? Anyone who earns the title of a critic has to have some claim to a synthetic talent above that of individual authors. The critic, in other words, has to be a genre expert, or at least be genre conscious. A critic must be able to place any work in a broader aesthetic context, at the very least, and also, usually, in a historical, an ethical, or some other higher context. And a genuine critic has to be reasonably even-tempered and fair-minded—or else so intriguing that he can get away with the occasional emotional outburst.

The way one becomes a respected critic is to manifest all these qualities over a long enough time so that one's readers are confident that they are in the presence of the real thing. Real critics are therefore fairly rare. Far more common are hacks posing as genuine critics, vulnerable to the criticism of others because they presumptuously judge art forms they themselves have not mastered. Thus the playwright Wilson Mizner once acerbically but fairly defined a drama critic as "a person who surprises a [writer] by informing him what he meant."

To my mind, the greatest twentieth-century American critic, a true man of letters, was Edmund Wilson. The writer Dorothy Parker, famous of the Algonquin Hotel crowd responsible for the *New Yorker* magazine back in the 1930s, is another example. Because Ms. Parker was so insightful, fair-minded, and reliable for so many years, she was able eventually to get away with writing things that lesser critics would never even have attempted. She once reviewed a book that was, in her opinion, so very bad that she wrote of it famously as follows: "This is not a novel to be tossed aside lightly. It should be thrown with great force."

Critics become their own object sometimes, and if they are great enough, as Wilson was, books about them will be written by academics and even by other critics. And then those books, in turn, get reviewed. So a review of a book about a critic—like an essay *The American Interest* once published by the contemporary critic Michael McDonald on a book about Edmund Wilson—is, properly speaking, a review of a review of a great man who was . . . a reviewer. Try to keep that in mind, no matter how much it hurts. This sort of thing does not add up to an infinite regress, but it comes about as close as any literary form does.

T here are many kinds of reviews. There are short reviews of single books, like those you find in the back of *Harper's* and many other magazines. Such reviews can be about fiction and nonfiction works, and about books that are boundary dwellers between fiction and nonfiction: *Snow,* a story of clashing cultures by the Turkish author Orhan Pamuk; or the Afghan coming-of-age tale *The Kite Runner* by Khaled Hosseini; or *The Satanic Verses,* the controversial "banned book" of 1989 by Salman Rushdie. By distinguishing fiction from nonfiction, and by mentioning boundary dwellers, I remind you not to ignore the politically persuasive power of fiction. From *Uncle Tom's Cabin* to *Brave New World* to *The Gulag Archipelago,* fiction can make a big difference in our presumably nonfiction world.

There are short reviews grouped in sections, usually written by one author. If you turn to the back of any issue of *Foreign Affairs*, you will see examples. In prestigious magazines of record like *Foreign Affairs*, those who lord over these sections of short reviews, sometimes for entire decades, accrue a fair amount of power. They become the equivalent of policy debate gatekeepers. It is also a rule of the review business that a bad review is better than no review of all, because it at least draws attention to the fact that the book exists.

It is also a rule of life more generally that a bad review of a book, if written by the right person, can be of enormous benefit to the author.

In the earlier chapter on essays we observed that different ideological persuasions use footnotes to indicate membership in or sympathy with a given school's point of view. If a known member of a certain school of thought is ripped to shreds by a reviewer from a contending ideological persuasion, then that author becomes a noble martyr in the eyes of likeminded associates. Those associates will then be far more likely to buy her book and possibly even read it. This is true of criticism more generally, as well. Harvard University history professor Richard Pipes once said that it is an honor to be disliked if one is disliked by the right sort of people (he had Nazis and Communists in mind). Very often, review essays of books with volatile political content are written versions of this general observation.

It goes almost without saying that many review essays are long rather than short. There are publications devoted entirely to review essays of this sort. The best examples are the *New York Review of Books* and the *Times Literary Supplement*. Because such publications tend to have ideological leanings of their own, which charm some but dismay others, publications with different views arise in the marketplace, like the *Claremont Review* with its conservative bent, for example.

Most publications that are devoted entirely or significantly to reviews often solicit and publish essays that take on two or more books at once. Many of these are the best sorts of review essays to be found, because they have made it acceptable for a prestigious reviewer to use the review as a platform for his own ideas. As long as the books are not entirely ignored, this form of review essay can bear much merit: Multiple book essays that express the reviewer's own ideas often have the virtue of placing the books in a broader context. They therefore align better with the literary majesty of true criticism.

As a rule, such multiple book projects begin with the reviewer speaking generally about the subject matter the books cover. In doing so, she might make points against which the books will subsequently be judged. Only after defining the breadth and significance of the subject matter is the first book introduced, described, and evaluated. The author may then return briefly to more general language before introducing, describing, and judging a second book, which may then be compared to the first. As you can see, a multiple book review offers an author a range of structural choices: A sagacious reader will concern himself not only with what is to be learned about the books under review but also with the broader subject matter at hand and the reviewer's skill at laying out both together in a comprehensive essay.

Scholars and serious policy analysts consider it an honor to be asked to write a multiple book review essay. No sentient editor will invite someone to craft such an essay unless that person is deemed capable of rising above ground level in their understanding of the books. And, again, experienced and sagacious readers will know that.

Note that footnotes can play a role in such review essays. Let us say that an editor collects three, four, or five books on a given subject—perhaps on the so-called Arab Spring, or conditions in contemporary Russia, or the 2012 presidential election campaign—but the reviewer comes to believe that one or two of the volumes simply don't measure up to the others in significance. The reviewer may then suggest that only the two or three key works be mentioned in the published review's title box and that footnotes be used to list and comment cursorily on the others. Oftentimes an editor who has not read every book and is not an expert on the topic will agree to this, the assumption being that the reviewer is in a better position to make such judgments. To be an ambitious author whose book rates only a footnote mention in a multiple book review essay by a prominent reviewer is a true disappointment. This represents a corollary and a partial exception to the general rule that a bad review is better than no review at all: Being mentioned as an also-ran in a footnote within a review essay can actually be worse than not being mentioned at all.

Short, long, and multiple book reviews do not even begin to exhaust the various forms of the review essay. Oeuvre reviews, for example, expose to the critic not one or many books at random, but the entire corpus of writing by a single author. Oeuvre reviews are thus a cross between review essays and biographies.

There are also what some in the field refer to as retroviews. A retroview is a review of an old book, or sometimes an old essay, in light of contemporary circumstances. Sometimes the book can be quite old. Anniversaries of publication may furnish the occasion for such retroviews. The year 2005 marked the centenary of the publication of Max Weber's famous essay on the Protestant ethic, so naturally there was heightened interest in how Weber's analysis stood up over the years. (It stood up rather well.) Sometimes the book can be far more recent in origin, yet circumstances will have changed enough since publication to warrant another look. It was interesting, for example, to review several books written back in the 1980s that predicted Japan overtaking the United States economically after it had become irrefutably clear that Japan had fallen into a deep and protracted economic stagnation. There is a natural curiosity about books and entire groups of books that end up having been obviously very wrong. Many readers enjoy such review essays for their marvelous capacity to evoke the delights of schadenfreude (a term I invite you to look up if you don't know its meaning).

The best thing about retroviews is that they allow for a particularly creative form of triangulation. Consider what is really happening when an author is composing such a review essay. Instead of there being merely two points of reference—a binary literary solar system, as it were—there may be and often are three. Take, for example, Edmund Burke's book about the French Revolution.[1] One point of reference is the Great Britain of Burke's time, a second Paris just months or a few years earlier, and a third that of our author. This allows an author to make observations in what amounts to three-dimensional literary–historical space. That opens up possibilities simply not available in a standard review essay.

It is often said that in comedy, timing is everything. There is much truth in that. But timing is also very important when it comes to writing review essays. Publications that come out often—newspapers that review books on a weekly basis, or magazines like *The Economist*—must be prompt in their coverage of newly published books. That is what readers expect of them and that is what they have become adept at doing. The editors of quarterlies or bimonthlies cannot compete with their more frequently published associates, but they can do something the faster-to-press cannot do: review a book along with reviews of it that have come out already. This sets up another kind of triangulation, and it allows a reviewer to attack or support a point of view that is not necessarily the author's, or the author's alone.

There are, within these categories of longer reviews, other ways to slice and dice the genre. Some reviews are favorable. Some are favorable but nitpick. A totally favorable review is sort of boring. One almost never finds them, and readers do not expect to find them. Some reviews are unfavorable, and some are unfavorable but, as Woody Allen says, "with an explanation." In other words, some reviews are unfavorable but written more in sorrow than in anger: "If only the author had . . ."

Some negative reviews get personal, violating Sidney Hook's maxim

---

1. Edmund Burke, *Reflections on the Revolution in France* (1790), edited and translated by L.G. Mitchell (New York: Oxford University Press, 1993).

that one should meet an argument before disparaging a person's motives. This reminds me that I have thus far neglected to address the how-to aspects of writing a review essay. The reason is twofold.

First, virtually all of the 12 rules of writing a good essay apply also to writing a good review. There is no need to repeat them all, except to note that a review can be and usually is a virtual debate or a form of debate in which the reviewer disagrees in some significant way with the author or authors being reviewed. In a normal essay, a writer can (if he so chooses) ignore the existence of different points of view. In a typical review essay, this is simply not possible. In a way, then, review essays are more honest, or at least more obvious, examples of ideological engagement when their subjects are political in character.

Second, I have said little of a how-to nature on review writing so far because this is one of those rare occasions when a firm understanding of the genre produces its own advice. What I have explained thus far focuses more on grasping the meaning, the function, and the overall power of the review essays you read than on crafting them from scratch. You need to know what given forms of review essays can do, and once you understand that from reading several of them, you will be able to undertake such projects yourself. You need to know the geometry of assertion, counter assertion, and counter–counter assertion that is natural both to review essays and to successions of review essays. And once you understand this geometry, you will be able to navigate it yourself. You need to become aware over time of the reasons why editors ask certain authors to review certain books, sometimes honestly and sometimes with malice aforethought; once your awareness has matured, you will be able to make your way among the thickets of colliding intentions. Let us continue, and you will see what I mean. I will deign to summarize all this for you in a simplified how-to section at the end of the chapter.

There are standard sins committed in reviews. One is that sometimes a reviewer will have such a firm idea about a subject that no author can possibly please him. This too often leads negative reviewers to castigate an author for either doing or not doing something she never claimed to do, or not do, as the case may be. Sometimes reviewers mistake an author's purpose, including specifically the audience she has selected. Some 20 years ago, Robert D. Kaplan wrote a book called *Balkan Ghosts: A Journey Through History.* The book became quite popular not least because President Bill Clinton let it be known that he had read it, and that he took to heart its arguments about the enduring ethnic conflicts in the Balkans. President Clinton understood the book as warning against precipitous American military intervention in the conflicts that exploded with the disintegration of Yugoslavia. Several reviewers, in turn, glared at Kaplan for influencing American policy in a direction they did not favor.

The irony was that Kaplan intended no such message for his readers, neither to the President nor to anyone else. He was quite chagrined at being criticized for a consequence he never intended. Soon another irony kept company with the first: The United States did eventually intervene militarily in the Balkans, not once but twice, and the enduring ethnic conflicts of the area have made some regret those interventions.

In the politics business, authors are known, and so are reviewers. And it happens, not infrequently, that tables get turned in the top-tier magazines and journals that host review essays. Many an editor will remember that a certain well-known writer used a review essay as a forum to criticize another well-known writer's new book. When that critic publishes a book of his own, you can lay odds that some editor will ask that ill-treated author to review his critic's new book. Editors love to do these things, because that's how to make sparks fly. That's how to attract readers.

Successful editors are not stupid; they are merely sometimes cynical. They know that people like gossip, and some know that gossip has its social uses as well as its seamier side. They know that people relish the personalization of political disagreements, even though no one and nothing is helped by it. Publishers are reluctant to let editors use cover images featuring piles of money, cute babies, or buffed-up bodies, even though these are proven ways to sell magazines, so they have to settle for personalized controversy instead. They remind one of Frederick II's description of Hapsburg Empress Maria Teresa on the occasion of the partition of Poland in 1772: "She wept and she wept, but she took and she took."[2]

Given the nature of political controversy and the personal dynamics it brings in its train, one thing honest editors should never do is accept unsolicited book reviews. The reason is that one cannot know for certain whether the author who suggests the review may have ulterior

---

2. Antonia Fraser, *Marie Antoinette: The Journey* (New York: Doubleday, 2001), p. 99.

motives for doing so. That person may want to pillory the author of the book or, alternatively, to praise him to the sky for reasons that have nothing to do with the quality of the book. An editor is duty bound in any case when he designs review essays to ask prospective reviewers if they know the author of the book to be reviewed, or if prospective authors have any financial relationship with the publisher of the book. An editor has to rule out the possibility of extraneous motives, or the exercise is something less than honest. So when someone approaches an editor with a proposal, the easiest thing to do is simply to say, no, that it is a policy of the magazine or journal not to accept unsolicited reviews for all the reasons just set down here.

Now, when a publisher comes to an editor and asks that a certain book be reviewed, and that the review come out in a certain way, this is called corruption. This has happened to me as an editor, and it is a most unpleasant situation in which to find oneself. So another piece of advice: If you can help it, do not work as an editor for a publisher whose integrity you do not respect.

Reviews, and publications that are all or mainly reviews, have become more influential lately, and not just in the United States. The reason, most agree, is that educated people cannot possibly keep up with everything of potential significance that is being published, so the best way to get an idea of what is out there is to read a few hundred or a few thousand words instead of tens and hundreds of thousands. I do it. Everyone I know in this line of work does it. In other words, people read reviews as filters. They do not necessarily trust the reviewer to render a judgment similar to their own, but they trust the reviewer enough to decide which of several dozen books they intend to make time to read.

Of course, it is true that lots of people use reviews not as filters but as substitutes for actually reading books. That's why it is so galling when a reviewer misunderstands and misrepresents an argument. It happens, though—sometimes out of malice, sometimes out of laziness, sometimes because an editor asks a reviewer to review material beyond his competence. Whatever the reason for it, when this happens and you know it has happened, you tend never to trust that reviewer again. You get to know people by reputation, and editors know this, too. So to be a successful reviewer—let alone to elevate oneself to the high status of a critic—you have to write more than just a few reviews, you have to be good, and you have to be fair; otherwise, a kind of natural selection will select you out of the reviewers' club.

The main and worst exceptions are in ideological, self-referential magazines. There, an editor picks books to review and matches them to reviewers because he knows the outcome in advance. This, too, is called corruption, or dishonesty if you like. Whatever you call it, it unfortunately happens all the time. When Kate O'Bierne's book *Women Who Make the World Worse* was published in 2005, it was reviewed in *National Review,* the magazine she worked for at the time. This was not good. No one expects a truly honest review in a situation like that, which is why at *The American Interest* I avoid assigning reviews to books published by members of the magazine's executive editorial committee. Naturally, the *National Review* reviewer loved Ms. O'Bierne's book, and just as naturally, a few days later a reviewer for the Sunday *New York Times Book Review* did a hatchet job on it, as everyone expected. Editors don't have to tell a reviewer to pan a book; they already know from their choice of reviewer how the thing is going to turn out, and the reviewer chosen knows the editor knows, and no one has to say a word to confirm the arrangement. All of this, of course, is a form of corruption, which is why it is so refreshing to come upon publications—and there are still many—that do not allow such things to mar their professionalism.

Now, reviews of this predictable sort can be entertaining, but they are not usually edifying or enlightening. The one thing that former Youth International Party, or Yippie, leader Jerry Rubin ever said that I completely agree with is that ideological thinking, the kind of "thinking" in which one's foreordained conclusion shapes one's thinking instead of the other way around, is a brain disease. If you happen to be an ideological thinker you can have great fun with hatchet jobs, just as true fans can enjoy a 19–2 drubbing in a baseball game if the right team is winning. But that does not make a hatchet job or a bad game something other than what it is. Your developing internal standards of excellence will help you understand that by and by.

Some things never change, it seems. It is just as it says in the book of Ecclesiastes 1:9: "There is nothing new under the sun." Except for when there is. Those who have been in the rhetoric and polemics business in one form or another for many years have noticed that there are fewer places where serious book review essays appear nowadays. Just as there is less investigative journalism in the newspaper, and just as the average length of news stories and magazine articles has grown shorter, so serious critical analysis of new literature is waning.

Some people think that the instant gratification characteristic of the blogosphere, and the much lower standards that reign there, are largely to blame. Others point out that the economics of print media have changed almost beyond recognition in just the past decade, especially in light of the corporate consolidation of the industry. The change is pervasive. Very large and profitable bookstore chains like Borders and Barnes & Noble suddenly found themselves bankrupt or nearly so at the hands of Amazon, which has undermined the viability of retail book store outlets. Magazines that rely largely on newsstand sales as opposed to subscriptions are hurt by the fall of Borders and the decline Barnes & Noble as well. Many magazines have gone out of business or have moved to electronic-only formats, and those forms have not been friendly to the art of the review essay. As the average length of all parts of electronic magazines has been reduced, the serious review essay is becoming an endangered species of the literary sort.

Where all this will lead, and with what consequences for a democratic public, no one knows. Something tells me that it's leading to nothing good. Maybe book review essays will not exist as a common form of literary art a decade from now. Maybe they will have gone the way of the eighteenth-century broadside, overtaken by styles and technology. Maybe books as we have known them will not exist either. The fact that a lot of book publishers have been losing their shirts in recent years may suggest as much.

In the meantime, however, you might still have to write a review, so here is a distillation of the most important advice that may be taken from the foregoing.

RULE 1: Be honest to the book. You owe your readers a fair description before you set off to criticize or praise. Remember that most readers of reviews these days use them as a filter or as a substitute for actually reading the book, so you cannot assume that the reader knows as much as you do about it. This means not only describing the author's thesis, but also the author's method and sources.

RULE 2: Avoid criticizing an author for not doing something he never set out to do. Don't impose your conception of the subject matter on an author. Evaluate what is, not what isn't. Let sins of commission be your main concern, and reserve sins of omission for a minor key.

RULE 3: Broaden the base of a review essay by setting the book or books into a proper context. That can include background information about the subject matter or reference to other books on similar subjects. But make sure that context does not overwhelm foreground; give the book its due.

RULE 4: Understand that if an editor asks you to write a multiple book review, or a retroview, you should consider it an honor. But recognize as well that doing these kinds of reviews proficiently is much more difficult than the standard fare. Accept the challenge, and then rise to the occasion.

RULE 5: Don't write a review and present it to the editor of a magazine unsolicited. As already noted, many magazines have policies against accepting unsolicited book reviews. You should know the magazine or journal for which you are writing or wish to write—know its style, its length parameters, its way of dealing with footnotes, and everything else pertaining to essays in general. But you should also know its policies about unsolicited reviews. When in doubt, ask the editor the proper way to proceed. If you inform an editor that you are interested in writing a review essay, that will not hurt your prospects.

RULE 6: Avoid ad hominem language. Meet and defeat an author's argument on intellectual grounds, if you think it deserves defeat, but do not impugn motives.

RULE 7: Remember that any unfairness or gratuitously impolite language you introduce in a review essay is very likely to come back to haunt you, especially if one day you ever write a book subject to the review of others. What goes around really does come around most of the time. Try to make sure it doesn't come around to you.

Recommended Reading

Jackson Diehl, "Fall Gal," *The American Interest,* Spring 2006.

Adam Garfinkle, "Set the Alarm for 2011," *New York Times Book Review,* February 4, 2001.

Gordon S. Wood, "Colonial Correctness," *The New Republic,* June 6 & 13, 2005.

In addition, familiarize yourself with the tables of contents of the current issues of the *New York Review of Books* and the (London) *Times Literary Supplement* (TLS).

Writing Exercise

Write a 500- to 700-word review of the lead essay or of the cover feature essay (they will not necessarily be the same) in the current issue of any major American monthly, bimonthly, or quarterly magazine.

6 THE OP-ED

Whatever becomes of the book review essay, the op-ed (a shortened form of "opposite the editorial page") has a long future ahead of it in one form or another. There will always be opinions, and enough time for the occasional rant. So on we go to the world of the op-ed.

Everything has a history, even the future. And of course that includes the op-ed. As with all the other topics in this book, it is my firm belief that before how-to advice can make any sense to you, you have to know something about the subject matter. So bear with me while we go over some critical background. This will not be painful, and besides, you might just learn something of interest.

What we know of as the daily newspaper, whether in its typical American form or in the form of European papers, got its start some five centuries ago—not all that long, really, as human history goes—after Johannes Gutenberg did his thing with movable type.

Gutenberg invented movable type around 1450. A man named Henry Caxton brought the first printing press to Britain in 1474. It then took about 50 years for the machine tools and commercial infrastructure to spread sufficiently to enable a basis for printing books and other kinds of things in any sort of large numbers. It so happens, too, that around the same time, as the late medieval period gave way to what historians call the early modern period, cities became larger and more prominent in the social life of Western and eventually Central Europe. With the growth of cities came the growth of literacy. So with more people who knew how to read, there was more demand for books and other printings such as calendars.

Moreover, at the eighteenth-century dawn of the Age of Reason—the Enlightenment as we like to call it—people began to separate the corpus of secular knowledge from the corpus of theology, to separate science from religion. (Of course, I am simplifying and summarizing dramatically.) The result was a diffusion of sources of social authority and interest; in short, as noted in Chapter 1, there were more subjects that could be written about, and more people interested and able to read about them. This combination of literate people, printing presses, larger and greater numbers of cities, and what we call today a more secular attitude toward learning in general created what we can call a literary culture of the sort we recognize today.

Note, too, that around this time we have the creation, or at any rate the maturation, of fictional literary forms. Henry Fielding's *Tom Jones*, one of the first English-language novels, did not appear until 1749. But long before that—indeed, nearly two centuries before that—legends, stories, and tales that had long been part of pre-Christian Europe's oral folk tradition were written down. So, for example, in the Teutonic world, Germany and Scandinavia, the legend of Siegfried and Brunhilde took literary form.

By the time Miguel de Cervantes wrote *Don Quixote de la Mancha* in Spain in the early seventeenth century, he could make fun of and use for a prop the tradition of stories written about chivalry and knights and related popular literature. *Don Quixote* itself, in the form it eventually took, shows the transition from theater into novels, for the first part of what we know today as *Don Quixote* was originally written as five related plays. When Cervantes finished the book as we know it today, more than a decade later, he went back and turned the plays into prose.

Obviously, writers like Cervantes and so many others who wrote in those times did so because there was a market for what they produced. You do not have playwrights and novelists without audiences, and you cannot have newspapers without readers who will buy them. And with readers who will pay comes the idea of advertising, and in early papers advertising usually took up a very large percentage of the space. Advertising circulars preceded newspaper as a print form in some places. For example, in early newspapers in the United Provinces (what we call today the Netherlands), the ratio of commercial announcements to news was about 90/10 for nearly two centuries after Gutenberg. And much of the "news" was comprised of proclamations by the government on this or that matter.

The idea of a "free press" that spoke to public issues was a while in developing, and it developed first, most maturely, and in some ways most astonishingly, in the English language—in Britain. It did so for several reasons. First, there was, of course, the Magna Carta of 1215. Political absolutism in Britain had limits in ways it did not have in most other places. In most places, absolute power—the tendency, as Ibn Khaldun famously said in the fourteenth century in *The Muqad-*

dimah, for political power to concentrate in the hands of one man—was checked by administrative limits. But in Britain these limits seem to have gained other rationales; no one quite knows why.[1]

Whatever its remote antecedents, a free press arose in Britain really more because of Martin Luther, John Calvin, and Henry VIII. It arose because the social needs of the time evoked it. The Reformation, and with it the particular attitudes of early Protestant Christianity, stressed the idea of personal individual moral agency, which it took from the Hebrew Bible and generalized into politics. The *individual* was the source, the true location of human agency, not the extended family, the community, or any other agglomeration of people. We see this elevation of the individual in more formal intellectual-philosophical terms later in Hobbes and Locke and others, and we see it in Montesquieu and others in France, too. But it was in Britain that the idea of individual agency was the strongest. It was especially in Britain that Protestants—Puritans, Anabaptists, Levelers, Diggers, and Lord-knows-who-else arose—insisted that true Christianity involved an unmediated relationship between the individual believer and God.

The early Protestants were also scripturalists, which means they believed that the text of the Bible was itself authoritative, and that all one needed to know to live a moral life could be derived from it. That put a huge premium on individual human moral agents knowing how to read. Scripturalists believed that the Catholic Church had diminished the power of scripture, substituting instead the accretions of the priesthood—a priesthood, they claimed, that had created rituals and beliefs with no basis in scripture. This priesthood, they further claimed, not without some good evidence, had gone out of its way to deny literacy to the masses of people.

Of course, by 1517, with Luther nailing his theses to the church door in Wittenberg, a lot of people could read. That made scripturalism possible. But scripturalism, in turn, fueled literacy. So the power of the written word was both *enabled* by Protestant scripturalism and greatly *extended* by it. The King James Bible, published in 1611, a little less than a century after Luther, then functioned as an accelerant of history on the crooked path to the modern op-ed. Aided by the proliferation of the King James Bible, British Protestants took a new attitude toward

---

1. An interesting examination of the British anomaly in this respect may be found in Francis Fukuyama, *The Origins of Political Order: From Prehuman Times to the French Revolution* (New York: Farrar, Straus and Giroux, 2011), chs. 27–28.

the printed word, and the many mysteries, ambiguities, and seeming contradictions within the biblical text naturally engendered arguments over the meaning of scripture. Many of these arguments began to take place with increasing frequency in writing. Sermons and polemics about sermonizers who disagreed with each other were among the first things that people wanted to read in print. So a whole corpus of religious literature, written in then-modern English, arose, and given the great energies of high- and low-church Protestants in England, and between Protestants and Catholics, a particularly energetic style of writing developed.

In Britain during this period, arguments over religion and arguments about politics were very closely connected, as anyone who is even vaguely aware of the history of Britain in the sixteenth and seventeenth centuries knows. What happened can be described fairly simply: Just as the linguistic energies of theater were transferred to the written word at a slightly earlier time, the character of religious polemic, sourced in scripturalism, transferred over easily to the new world of political polemic.

Those political energies were, in turn, picked up and translated back into theater, creating for the first time truly modern theater—that is, theater divorced from religious themes and concerns. Here exactly is where Christopher Marlowe and the great one, the Bard, William Shakespeare himself, come in.

These men, and a few others, were not just great; they were innovatively great. They were cultural-intellectual pioneers of the highest order, as any reading of Shakespeare's tragedies, compared to the theater fare of just a century before, shows. They bridged the conceptual shift from soul to self, and they pioneered the political uses of history in polemic as none before had done. If you need yet another example of how fiction powerfully wends its way in and out of political life, you need look no further than Shakespeare. And if Shakespeare is too rich for your blood, you can refer to Jonathan Swift, whose allegorical *Gulliver's Travels*, published in 1726, marks the beginning of genuine modern political literature. It is one the greatest books ever written in the English language, but if you know nothing of the history from which it springs and that provides its political context, you simply cannot understand what Swift is doing. You can still enjoy the story and its marvelous imagery, but you can understand it only at a superficial level.

A key figure in the middle of all this history as regards newspapers and op-eds, active about equidistant in years between Shakespeare and

Swift, was a wild and strange fellow named Marchamont Nedham (1620–1678). Nedham was the favorite journalist of England's lord protector, Oliver Cromwell. In fact (notice, please, the extremely rare use of "in fact" in my writing), Nedham was the first modern journalist. Here is how he explained why he became a newspaperman: "I tooke up my pen for disabusing his Majesty . . . and for taking off vizards and vailes and disguises." Nedham wanted to offend and he was, indeed, deeply offensive. He wanted to provoke and he succeeded; he was the first professional inky rebel provocateur.[2] He taught all English-speaking people who love liberty that offensiveness is the very touchstone of liberty, and that without it there is no meaningful freedom of expression.

Nedham wrote what was, in essence, the first op-ed, although in those days political diatribes were often several thousand words long, not just several hundred. Indeed, the op-ed extended really *was* the newspaper. It was in those days called a newsbook, the first of which was published on November 29, 1641, just on the eve of the English Civil War. So just as song probably preceded speech, so the op-ed in its original form as a political pamphlet preceded the newspaper. Again we note that particular forms of political expression arise out of complex social and political patterns. To explain our way to Marchamont Nedham, we need some mixture of technical advance (the printing press), economic change (growth of cities), social development (the advent of mass literacy), religious culture (the Reformation and English Scripturalism), and political upheaval: the English Civil War, Oliver Cromwell, and the Restoration of the monarchy. That is what, together, it took to pave the way to the first modern op-ed.

Or rather, the editorial. At first, owners of newspapers wrote opinions, and others were neither permitted nor expected to do so in their pages. So the editorial and the op-ed were in effect the same thing. Only much later did the idea of inviting outsiders, with potentially different views from those of the publisher, into one's pages arise. That is, strictly speaking, an op-ed, and that is what separates the left side of the opinion page from the right.

Today there are two kinds of op-edists: Columnists who are regulars, and guest writers who are not. So the editorial and the column and

---

2. For more on Nedham, see Paul A. Rahe, "An Inky Wretch: The Outrageous Genius of Marchamont Nedham," *The National Interest* (Winter 2002).

the op-ed are similar, but not exactly the same. Editorials state the paper's line, or the magazine's line if it has one, as the case may be. Columnists are usually deliberately diverse as a lot, but generally lean toward the editorial line of a particular newspaper. Op-edists are selected in such a way that they do, too. This means that there will always be some op-eds in any give week that will not align with the newspaper's editorial views. For example, a few years ago Francis Fukuyama and I co-authored an op-ed in the *Wall Street Journal* critical of the Bush administration, despite the fact that that newspaper defended the administration more vigorously than any other major paper in the country.[3]

But, as I have said, the three forms—editorials, columns, and op-eds—are similar enough that the rules which apply to any one of them apply more or less to all three types. What rules? How does one write a good op-ed? I bring you the thirteen points of counsel to guide the development of your skills.

RULE 1: Keep it short. If you do not keep it short, an editor will, and it is better for you to make those choices than for someone whose interests and knowledge might be different and less focused than your own to do so. More important, perhaps, if you do not keep it short, most editors will not even consider publishing it. They are busy people, so they look for material that can be easily readied for publication.

What is the definition of short when it comes to an op-ed? Seven hundred words is about right. Some newspapers will allow a bit more, and you can tell rather easily simply by counting the words in the average op-ed in the paper you wish to publish your work.

RULE 2: Limit yourself to one and only one significant argument or main point. You must deploy rigorous principles of exclusion from the very beginning in your conception of the piece of writing you mean to produce. If less is more generally in writing, it is excruciatingly true in op-ed writing. Every word must carry water. But more important for op-eds, less is more also in terms of content. If you try to do too much in a short space, you will end up doing nothing.

RULE 3: You must *have* a point, and it has to be in some way novel or unexpected. Newspaper editors in charge of the op-ed page see

---

3. The piece was called "A Better Idea," *Wall Street Journal*, March 27, 2006.

literally hundreds if not thousands of submissions every week. Since editors are in the business of pleasing publishers, and publishers are in the business of selling newspapers so that they can charge enough for advertisements to keep them in business, editors naturally incline to print op-eds they think people will read. This means that they are in search of op-eds tied to subjects that are controversial and current.

The point at the very center of your op-ed must not only be about these kinds of subjects, that point must be one that stands out from the debate. One way to do that is to state an extreme view, but this is a cheap and generally unhelpful contribution to debate—unless of course you genuinely take an extreme view. Another way, almost invariably a better way, to do this is to present your idea in counterintuitive fashion. Yet another way is to fix on a particular piece of terminology that is being thrown around in a careless fashion, and unpack it in such a way as to make an unexpected point. And yet another way to do this, among very many, is to introduce a key datum or fact of which readers are unaware, but that casts a new light on the broader subject.

RULE 4: Even if your subject is controversial and current, you need to pay special attention to crafting a hook at the very beginning of the piece. This can be a straight news hook or it can be some other kind of attention-arresting statement. A particularly vivid quotation from some character deep in the middle of the story can work. So can a particularly revealing statistic. The point is that you must have a hook of some kind because readers, these days especially, are very particular about being bored. They are far more likely to read through a piece of writing that piques their curiosity then they are one whose appeal is mottled by an indistinct beginning.

RULE 5: Communicate the essence of your argument in the first paragraph, preferably in the last sentence of a short first paragraph. Readers of op-eds are repulsed not only by a prospect of boredom, but also by a prospect that a piece of writing might waste their time. Luckily, the subculture of expository writing in English is suited well to this demand. There are other cultures, the Russian for example, in which the typical way of telling a story is to begin with small islands of coherence and then in the end bring them all together to establish the point of the narrative. In American English, we tend more often to alert readers of what is about to happen by giving away the essence at the start. This is the approach that must be followed rigorously in an op-ed.

RULE 6: Compose at least some pithy short sentences. Ideally, there should be at least one easily quotable phrase that captures and carries the entire effort. It can be very difficult to come up with this phrase, but you must try your best to do it. It might take time, but then you will be writing at least 8 to 10 drafts of this effort before you are finished, before you have attained your internal standard of excellence. Devoting that much thought to the subject is the key to finding the magical phrase you need. Your magical phrase might even be, or contain, a neologism. Most likely, it will just suddenly come to you after a good sleep.

RULE 7: In an op-ed, it is appropriate, depending on your subject, to use irony (but not sarcasm), wit (but not cynicism), paradox, and metaphor. At least one of these, it is safe to say, is required for an op-ed to be truly excellent.

RULE 8: The use of one-sentence paragraphs, totally off-limits in an essay of any form, is allowed in an op-ed. A one-sentence paragraph serves one purpose and one purpose only: drama. It draws attention to itself and it tacitly boasts to a reader: I am about to shake your world, and I am about to do it very economically. What this means is that if you deign to use a one-paragraph sentence, it had better be a dilly.

If you develop a regular newspaper reading habit, which you should, and if you regularly peruse the op-ed pages, you will find examples of excellent one-paragraph sentences. But just to save you the trouble for now, consider this one, which I have plucked out of one of the best op-eds I have ever seen; it is by Alan Ehrenhalt: "We need to be careful, or we will drive our best hypocrites out of public life."[4]

RULE 9: Use facts judiciously. A piece of short writing such as an op-ed is not a didactic exercise. There is no point in stating facts just because they are true. The reason to use facts is that they lend serious-

---

4. Alan Ehrenhalt, "Hypocrisy Has Its Virtues," *New York Times*, February 6, 2001.

ness, gravity, and therefore legitimacy to the argument you are making. If the facts you choose do not served this purpose, do not use them.

RULE 10: Give your op-ed a clear structure and flow. Your transitions must be perfect. The logical link between the last sentence of any paragraph and the first sentence of the next is especially critical. If you lose the reader once in an op-ed, you have lost her forever.

RULE 11: Use quotations, novel definitional language, neologisms, and aphorisms strategically—but use them. However, use at most two of these instruments per op-ed; usually just one is best. Think of these tools of the rhetorical trade as whipped cream or black truffle oil: They can be exquisite in small quantities, but they drown everything else out when they are overdone.

RULE 12: As with an essay, the first and last sentences are the most important and the hardest to write. So if you write 10 drafts of the rest of the op-ed, you may need to make 15 to 20 attempts to get the first and the last sentences exactly right.

RULE 13: As with all forms of persuasive writing, know which audience you are targeting. You may want to strengthen the morale of your own camp or piss off the opposition. You won't convert anyone in such a short space, but you can make people think, or worry. Since the form is limited, so must be your aspirations for it.

There is a second way to mean "know your audience" in the op-ed writing business. In addition to knowing your readers, you have to know your editors and newspapers. The *Wall Street Journal*, for example, likes more facts and denser "reportage" in op-eds than do other major papers. Some things you may wish to write lend themselves better to some newspapers than to others, and it is your job to know which are which.

Finally, note that trying and failing to place op-eds is not free. You may think, "Well, I have nothing to lose if the editor doesn't like this," and you would be quite wrong. If you repeatedly rush your efforts, failing to meet your internal standards of excellence in a blaze of emotional ebullience, you risk developing a reputation as someone who cannot meet the standards of a particular newspaper. If that happens to you, you will eventually suffer from irascible editors who are predisposed to judge harshly whatever you send, even if in the fullness of time you send something truly excellent.

The same is true, of course, for trying to place longer pieces of writing in magazines. If you pester editors with substandard work over and over again, you will do yourself no favors. This is why, as I have already tried to persuade you, the development of your own internal standards of excellence is so crucial to success at persuasive writing.

Recommended Reading

All the op-eds in any major American paper this week.

Hodding Carter, Jr., "Jesse Owens' Picture," *Delta Star*, July 16, 1937.

Alan Ehrenhalt, "Hypocrisy Has Its Virtues," *New York Times*, February 6, 2001.

Fred Hiatt, "Justice Best Served—Internationally: War Crimes Sanctimony," *Washington Post*, June 19, 2000.

R.J. Samuelson, "Greenhouse Hypocrisy," *Washington Post*, August 24, 2005.

Writing Exercise

Write an op-ed that has something to do with your present intellectual passion, maximum 700 words. (If you don't have an intellectual passion, that could be a problem in completing this assignment, and not only in completing this assignment.)

7 SPEECHWRITING

It is of course possible for political speeches to be written by the person who is actually going to give the speech. This used to be common in America, as well as elsewhere. Remember Abe Lincoln and the Gettysburg Address, for example, when the President supposedly scribbled his intended message on the back of an envelope as he was traveling to the site? Today, at least in the United States, this is very rare. Speeches usually are written from combined efforts involving the principal, a speechwriter, and often a host of additional intermediaries. That, anyway, is my grounding assumption in this chapter.

It is easy to discuss speechwriting in theory and in general, but like most things, in practice it is much harder to actually do.[1] The best place to start explaining the task is by contrasting a speech with an essay.

An essay has words and music. That is to say, it has lexical content and it has rhythm or cadence. We have already noted the critical role that rhythm plays in language, even making the point, as I did earlier, that in human evolution song preceded speech—to which we can now add the observation that in human civilization poetry may have preceded prose.

Now, if an essay has words and music, a speech has words, music, and dance steps. It is a three-dimensional form, compared to merely two for a written product. A speech is a species of performance art. It is, by definition, delivered live. Yet the writing of a speech must be accompanied by a sense of pretending that all the while one is writing it, the speaker is speaking it. Speechwriting is therefore more like what a playwright does than any other form of writing. One is writing for the purpose of someone else's speaking, and that changes everything.

It means, for example, that many of the rules one learns and wisely follows in writing essays and op-eds do not apply in writing speeches.

---

1. There is at least one text devoted to political speechwriting, written by Al Gore's former speechwriter. See Robert A. Lehrman, *The Political Speechwriter's Companion: A Guide for Writers and Speakers* (Washington, DC: CQ Press, 2009).

For example, the law of brevity, that less is more, applies in speech-writing, but differently. For an essay, you would never write a group of sentences like this: "The challenge before us is great. The challenge before us is unprecedented. And the challenge before us will nevertheless be met." No, you would write instead, "The challenge before us, though it is great and unprecedented, will nevertheless be met," or something like that. That is shorter and, as a thought expressed, clearer as well as more succinct. But in a speech, repetition is good; it is useful. It works.

Remember: When a person can read something, he can go as quickly or as slowly as he likes. A reader can go back over something. A reader can stop reading, get up for a snack or a bathroom break, and come back. Not so in a speech. To listen to language is to be told a story. A speech rests in the oral tradition, not in the written one. So to drive home a point, to make sure the audience is influenced the way the principal wishes to influence it, all sorts of mnemonic devices are in bounds that one would never use in a written work.

Another example of the different rules that apply to the writing of speeches as opposed to the writing of essays concerns lists. In an essay, lists are usually bad. In a speech, using numbers, as in, for example, "I have three points to make," helps to orient the listener to what is to follow. Formulations that constitute throwaway language in an essay— "If you will indulge me, I will dwell a bit longer on this particular point than usual" and other phrases of that sort—may be used in a speech. They should *always* be thrown away in an essay. The reason is that, although everyone in the audience knows that the speaker is using a text, a speech must nevertheless sound as spontaneous and natural as possible. So language like that is not only acceptable, it is good— depending on the venue and purpose of the speech.

But let's get back to dance steps. What do I mean by that? I mean that every speech is attended by body language, by what are known technically as paralinguistic cues. The tilt of the head, the look in the eyes, particularly the use of the hands and arms—they are all part of a speech. They not only allow emphasis to be placed; they make meaning. Even silence, the pause, can make meaning and produce emphasis.

Again, this is impossible to do in an essay. You can put ten ellipses spaces after a sentence and you still won't make a reader pause. But in a speech, you can put "pause here" in parentheses, and the speaker will pause; and when that happens, you as speechwriter and he as principal together will have done something that cannot be done in normal writing. As in comedy, where timing is everything, in a speech timing is maybe not everything, but it's a lot.[2]

Paralinguistic cues are tied to personality. A political principal is often a person with a reputation and a person who carries a certain aura. Much of the time, those present for a speech, or those who are watching it being delivered on C-SPAN or listening on the radio, already know the speaker—not personally, but as a public personality. That person has an image; so there are certain expectations built into a speech even before it begins. Often there is preexisting respect or loathing. A speechwriter must know this, and work this, and protect this, and consider all this when preparing a speech text. Again, it is a little like writing a play, particularly in a situation where the playwright knows the actors who are going to speak the parts. A political speech, however, is usually not Act I, Scene I when you are writing for a well-known person. It is somewhere in the middle of the play, and what has come before, as the audience is likely to perceive it, is critical to the speech's effectiveness.

Now, the most important thing about speechwriting, in the form we are discussing it here, is that it is words, music, and dance—but for someone else. Speechwriting is a form of "speaking in tongues," only it's someone else's tongue. So you have to really know that person. You have to get inside his head and gain a sense of what it is like to be that person. Like a playwright, again, or a screenwriter, you have to know the actor. You have to be a Zelig; see Woody Allen's 1983 movie *Zelig* and you will understand perfectly what I mean.

I would be less than honest, and less than compassionate, if I did not tell you that not everyone can do this. Just as some people are tone deaf, some can't mimic foreign accents, some can't achieve verbal fluency, and some can't reimagine historical frameworks, some people cannot embody other personalities. And so, at a certain level, speechwriting is a skill that cannot be taught except to a modest degree. But it's crucial: If you cannot perceive the patterns of speech of the person for whom you are writing, you will present that speaker with impossible

---

2. When I taught this course, I used as part of my package of preparatory materials actual videos of Secretary of State Colin Powell delivering speeches I had written for him. You can watch a whole range of political speeches on C-SPAN, YouTube, and so forth. You should, as accompanying material to the readings listed at the end of the chapter.

problems. You will use vocabulary they do not choose, and you will devise cadences with which they are not comfortable. The result is that the speaker will seem ill at ease and lacking in spontaneity, and if the speaker is ill at ease with his text, he will not be persuasive with the audience. Persuasiveness, after all, is the point.

Last in respect to the dynamics of delivery, if a speech is to seem natural to an audience upon delivery, the text—which, again, everyone knows is there, somewhere—has to seem invisible. Every principal who is experienced with giving speeches likes her text set out in a certain way. Most prefer simple type, without serifs and do-dads of any kind. Ariel is a favorite of many. The type should be large and bold. And you should never allow what are known as "widows" onto the page. A widow is a fragment of a sentence that rolls over onto the next page. Every page should end with a full sentence.

Every page should also end only two-thirds of the way down the sheet. Why is this? Imagine a speaker standing behind a dais, with the text on a slanted surface hidden from the audience, with a light above it. (That's how it usually is.) The speaker, wishing to speak to the audience in a manner that appears as natural as possible, achieves that effect in very large part by looking at the audience—making eye contact. If you fill in a speech text page to the bottom, you as speechwriter force the speaker to dip her chin and bring her eyes lower than she should to give the impression of keeping eye contact. That's why.

A speechwriter cannot do everything for a speaker. The speaker has to have some skills, as well. Colin Powell is a master at this. He knows how to use hand motions just as he is about to move a page, so that no one in the audience ever sees him manipulating paper. The viewers' eyes follow the right hand, say, as the left is uncovering page eight and covering page seven. It is a dance step of sorts.

Some speakers like their pages loose. Some like them in a little notebook, with the inner corners of the sheets cut off so they do not rustle when turned and so make noises that a microphone will pick up. If you are writing a speech for a relative novice, say, in the House of Representatives, that speaker has a lot to learn about giving speeches that has nothing to do with substance, and a savvy speechwriter can teach that novice a lot.

But what help is there for novice speechwriters? How did I learn to write speeches for Colin Powell, and then for Condoleezza Rice? I did what all good speechwriters do, as seniors in the craft more experienced than myself advised me to do: I studied them. I read Powell's autobiography, three times. I watched tapes of earlier speeches. I talked at length to Larry Wilkerson, then State Department chief of staff, who wrote speeches for Powell when the latter chaired the Joint Chiefs of Staff. I had speeches I wrote for him taped and I studied them carefully, looking for where Powell may have stuttered or winced. I did the same for Secretary Rice. I read previous speeches I knew she liked. I watched her. I listened to her. I spent hours doing this. When I had "face time" with her, I watched her body motion as she spoke. And when I brought a new speechwriter onto the Secretary's staff, I insisted he do the same. It's not enough to be a good writer, or even enough to be able to match words and music—to be a lyricist, as it were. You have to match it all to the principal. *You have to know your principal.*

Now, frankly, this can get a little weird sometimes. Everyone knows, including the principal, that you sometimes have to say things in a policy speech that do not necessarily come naturally to people. Powell is extraordinarily intelligent, but he does not think of himself as an intellectual. He doesn't particularly trust abstract language. Four-star generals are operational types, and people like that often develop a kind of tough faux proletariat veneer—especially Army officers and Marines (Air Force and especially Navy types, I've found, are often different). But Powell fully understood that sometimes he needed to use abstract language, that as Secretary of State he had to say certain things to certain audiences that did not roll naturally out of his mouth. That is what I tried to help him do. And to hear those kinds of words, *my* words, come out of *his* mouth was really an out-of-body experience, especially the first few times I experienced it. It is, for the speechwriter, completely exhausting.

I had a dear friend who worked as a speechwriter for not one but three Secretaries of State. He told me that he found listening to the delivery of a speech he had written, especially one delivered by Secretary of State George Shultz, was an excruciating experience. He told me that he could barely walk for an hour after the first time he did this. So disconcerting was it that he vowed never to be in the audience again during such a performance.

This person had a vivid sense of humor, and so I thought he was just kidding around—until the same thing happened to me. The first major speech I wrote for Secretary Powell was delivered at Lisner Auditorium on the campus of George Washington University in Washington, DC. It was Powell's first major policy speech as Secretary of State, one that he and everyone else appreciated was overdue. The speech naturally drew national and international press. (I reworked slightly the text of the speech in due course and it became the lead essay in an issue of *Foreign Affairs.*[3]) We worked very hard to get this right. I had even gone out to Powell's home to discuss it on one occasion. We were both very pleased with the final text, and he delivered it brilliantly. But there I was, in about the tenth row, perspiring heavily and shaking lightly in my shoes. At one point, I started silently mouthing the words, which of course I had memorized, as Powell was speaking, leading the person to my left to act in a visibly uncomfortable manner. By the time the thing was over, I could barely walk. I vowed never to sit in the audience again for a major address, and I didn't.

So let's sum up what we know so far about the "dark arts" of speechwriting:

- Speechwriting is a performance art, with dance as well as words and music.
- Speechwriting defies many of the rules that apply to other kinds of persuasive writing.
- Speechwriting is speaking in tongues, so you must know your principal; you must capture and project his voice.

But there is more, much more.

A great political speech has six key elements, and if you aspire to write one, these elements may be expressed as rules.

RULE 1: Enmesh your speech text in a sacred narrative of some kind. To persuade, you must raise and direct emotion. The best way to do that in politics is to evoke what is sacred within a given political culture. This almost always depends on identifying and deploying the right condensation symbols—symbols that conjure up multiple meanings, usually of a complex and emotional nature—and the right ones depend on both the occasion and the reputation of the speaker. Do you think that writing for two black U.S. Secretaries of State had its advantages? Could I use Abraham Lincoln, Ralph Bunche, and Martin Luther King, Jr., in ways I could never get away with had I been writing for others? You bet I could, and I did.

---

3. Colin L. Powell, "Power and Principle," *Foreign Affairs* (January 2004).

RULE 2: Restrict yourself to just one key message for the listener to take home. This is not a stricture one is bound to in expository writing; in an essay, readers can absorb a certain level of complexity by pondering and rereading a text. A speech, on the other hand, must be pre-structured to sink into the memory of a listener. Therefore, the purpose of the speech must be the speechwriter's guidepost from the outset, and a speechwriter must be able to summarize that purpose in one sentence. Once the principal knows that purpose and tells the speechwriter, everything else must be devoted to getting that aim accomplished, notwithstanding the many other considerations and distractions that accompany the speechwriting process.

And remember, the purpose is to persuade, or to reassure, or to create a feeling of security. It is not to teach. A political speech is not a didactic exercise. It is far more like a sermon than a lecture. Therefore, as I have already indicated, and as was taught to me by a master, *never commit a gratuitous truth in a speech*. Never have your principal say something just because it's true and interesting. If it doesn't play a role in persuasion and purpose, leave it out.

RULE 3: Keep the structure of the speech simple. In outline form, it must never have more than one subset of points. Violate this structure and you will have created a speech that will be too hard for listeners to follow. A speech must never come across as a perpetual parenthetical, as a kind of infinite regress. If you lose the audience, ever, just once, your speech is not great. It will not even be good.

RULE 4: Not only must your structure be simple, you must match it to the melodic flow of the substance. In other words, in a 20-minute speech designed to make one point, you cannot have a structure that is more complex than the purpose warrants. If you plan a 45-minute speech that has some unavoidably technical or didactic aspects to it, then you can, and really you must, make the speech's structure a little more ornate. The point is that there must be a proper correspondence between the simplicity or complexity of the message and the form that message takes.

RULE 5: Give the speech's text an even tone. If you start solemn, stay solemn. If you start informal and witty, stay that way. Only a true master, a real genius, can bounce around changing styles. It doesn't work for most people, and an uneven tone in a speech can be a killer. A switch of tone that is too abrupt can bounce a listener out of frame, breaking the spell of persuasion in the process.

RULE 6: Give the speech's text drama. Make it move along in such a way that the listener doesn't get lost, as I've said, but also in a way that the listener doesn't know what's coming. A speech that is too predictable cannot be great.

But a speech depends on more than its text, and on more than a principal's skilled delivery of it. When I use the phrase "breaking the spell," I really mean it. Like all performance art, certain conventions define where the activity of a speech starts and where it ends, what it encompasses and what it does not. There is a branch of sociology and social psychology that speaks best to this issue: it is called phenomenology. We will not indulge those insights now except to say that we human beings can do amazing things with our brains. What is the reality status of a play? Of a play within a play, as in Shakespeare's *A Midsummer Night's Dream*? How do we stay engrossed in a fictive presentation? If we are forever calling attention to the conventions that allow us to do this, we can't stay engrossed. These are some of the questions a phenomenological approach asks.

To illustrate better what I mean and why this matters, let me relate that there used to be (maybe there still is) something called the theater of the absurd in which the playwright directed the actors to deliberately break the framing conventions of theater as part of its experimental method. Actors would sometimes arise from the middle of the audience. Members of the audience would be chosen at random, taken on stage, and asked to enter the play. The lighting and sound devices typically hidden from the audience's view would be revealed. The point was to integrate the framing conventions of the activity into the activity itself in an act of acute methodological self-consciousness. Audiences got tired of this sort thing pretty fast, but the same principles apply to a speech as a species of performance art. If certain framing conventions are broken, the power of the drama is destroyed. Deliberately breaking the frame by calling attention to it is exactly what hecklers do, of course. The importance of framing conventions also explains why things most people in the audience never even think about—like subtle changes in lighting, the backdrop behind the speaker, or how a room is arranged—can matter enormously.

The fact that listeners are gathered together in a room makes a huge difference, as well. Crowds have a psychology of their own, and you know—though you have probably never actually thought about it—that political speeches are never given to just one or two people. Did you ever consider the significance of this on how a speech is received? The size of the room and the number and kind of people in it are crucial. We are social animals, and our cognitive apparatus functions differently when we are assembled in large groups than when we are by ourselves or with just one or two other people.

To take a very simple example of this observation, it is a well-known rule in the political and diplomatic world that if a principal is speaking to a room of people where there are no chairs, the maximum length of the speech can be no more than 15 to 20 minutes. I have seen this rule of thumb broken on several occasions, and it is a grievous sin. People can forgive a lot, especially if they like the speaker, but being made to stand in one place longer than is comfortable is harder to forgive than you might expect.

But more than that, a small number of people in the room—say less than 30—will give a room a feeling of informality, so much so that a principal using a text in that circumstance will seem out of place. Experienced people sense when it is proper and improper to use a text. The first time I prepared a text for Secretary Powell in a situation where the room struck him as suitable for only an informal presentation, he did not use my exact text, but rather paraphrased aspects of it and got across the main message in what seemed to be an extemporaneous presentation. This hurt my feelings, because I had worked hard on that speech. He sensed my reaction, and after the session was over he walked into my office and told me that the situation was not right for a formal text-based presentation; however, he also made sure I understood that had I not prepared the text and had he not studied it, he would not have been able to give the presentation he did.

So speech texts can serve more than one purpose. The speechwriter does not become irrelevant when a principal decides to depart from a text, but the relevance changes. Indeed, the premium put on clarity and clean structure becomes even more important in such circumstances.

Maybe the best model for a great speech is a great short story, because in a way that's what a speech is. A great short story does the following, and generally does it in this order: (1) It sets the stage and then quickly introduces the mystery or tension that defines the plot. (2) It introduces additional characters and develops all characters. (3) It deepens the plotline as one goes, building to crescendo. (4) Finally, it gracefully implements denouement and resolution.

Obviously, in a political speech you have to be a little creative here.

Characters, for example, are rarely individuals, but are rather nations or sometimes even ideas. But you get the point.

So, there you have it, altogether, as follows:

- You're doing performance art, so follow rules of oral, not written, presentation.
- Know your principal.
- Enmesh your effort in a sacred narrative.
- Know and be guided by your purpose and message.
- Keep your structure clean and proportional to the purpose.
- Keep your tone even.
- Mind the need for drama, and find the mean between clarity and unpredictability.

That's it. That's how you write a great speech.

Of course, in government and in other large organizational settings, there are subsidiary considerations—so many that, in truth, keeping yourself focused on what you are *really* doing is not always easy. A speechwriter, for example, cannot just make up policy, whether government, corporate, or institutional. You have to know what the policy is and stick to it. You often have to be repetitive, which is no fun for the speechwriter or the principal. The presence of "deliverables" in a speech simplifies the writing process considerably. A deliverable is a message that carries a new policy into the public light—that it vows to spend money, to make structural changes in government design, or, probably above all, that it threatens or announces the use of force. Speeches with deliverables almost write themselves (which doesn't mean they can be genuinely great without applying the points of art discussed here).

Seemingly little things matter a lot, too. Grace notes are critical. (Grace notes are the introductory please-and-thank-you language that acknowledges the person who introduces the principal, praises the organization or institution that invited him, and so forth.) You have to get them right. You may think of this as just the entrance ramp to the real speech, and of course it is, but if you screw up the grace notes—say, by mispronouncing someone's name that everyone in the audience knows, or by trying to pronounce an audience-endearing foreign-language word or phrase and butchering it—it folds the social air in all the wrong ways. The speaker sometimes never recovers to get his footing completely right.

There are also certain dangers that accompany a speaker's fame. I never experienced this problem with Secretaries Powell or Rice, but some principals like to drone on, beyond or outside of their texts. They think that because they are household names, people want to hear as much of their "wisdom" as possible. This tends to be the case more with elected officials than with public figures who rose from within the ranks of the military or the university. It is rarely true that audiences hang on every word, no matter how many words there are, and you must not let your principal drone on if you can help it. Every word must still do work. Busy, influential, and prestigious people must never be seen to be backfilling and wasting other people's time. It banalizes their reputation.

It is also important for speechwriters working for those who hold political office at any level to respect the authority of the office. There are some kinds of comments that are just not presidential or secretarial or senatorial. Remember that your principal is part of a system of government, and that other principals make speeches, too. So you have to coordinate from time to time. Some administrations are better at this than others, and some cabinet departments are more used to cooperating than others. I remember an occasion when Secretary Powell was going to be at an event at which the U.S. Treasury Secretary would also be present, and both of them were scheduled to make short speeches. It seemed to me only natural that I call the speechwriter responsible for Secretary John Snow's speech at this event. I wanted to make sure that the two speeches did not overlap excessively and that they were deconflicted with regard to certain sensitive issues before it was too late. After I finally got in touch with the speechwriter from the Treasury Department and explained to her who I was and what I wanted, the phone on her end seemed to go dead for a little while. When she eventually spoke, she explained to me that, in her experience, no one from the State Department had ever called anybody at the Treasury Department for any such reason. And she had been there for 22 years.

Also, when you are writing speeches for public figures, you know in the back of your head that the speech will be read as well as listened to upon live delivery. It will be read in the hours and days after delivery, and depending on the speaker and the occasion, it may be read years or even decades later by other officials and historians. So while a speechwriter's main task is acing the performance art event at which the speech is given, it is also to anticipate how the speech will sit within the broader record that future readers will peruse.

Another pitfall that speechwriters in large organizations must navigate is that from time to time certain of your colleagues just won't leave you alone. You may have a fine relationship with your principal, but in a government organization, whether it is the State Department, the Defense Department, the Senate, or the staff of a congressional representative, there will invariably be competition among staff for the ear of the boss. There will be disagreements about policy, and there will be disagreements about tactics. This is not because people are necessarily underhanded (though some certainly are); it is because they care about outcomes. Since you, as speechwriter, hold the almighty pen, some staff may try to end-run their competition by going directly to you in an attempt to influence how you craft a speech—because a speech actually has the power to make policy. Do not let them do this.

I remember once, flying on Air Force II with Secretary Rice, trying desperately to type out a speech on a laptop en route to India, when one of the Secretary's senior advisers came over to where I was sitting to see what I was doing. He knew perfectly well what I was doing. I knew perfectly well that he knew perfectly well what I was doing, and I knew what he was doing, too. He asked to take my laptop for a few moments so that he could type in a particularly wonderful line for the Secretary to deliver a few days hence in Tokyo. I could have said simply, "No, I don't think so." Instead, I quickly made a copy of my file and gave him the computer. He typed not one sentence, as promised, but at least a half dozen. When he gave me back my laptop, I recognized the subject matter on which he wrote as one of disagreement among several members of the Secretary's staff. I simply deleted his intervention and got back to work.

This anecdote illustrates a final point. Depending on the principal, a speechwriter has a certain amount of power. Who holds the pen, ultimately, can in effect make policy because the writer often becomes by default an arbiter of conflicting advice and views. A writer, if he is part of the policy process, can also have a crucial formative impact on a policy speech in the way he structures the subject. I have been in that position, but modesty and certain security protocols prohibit me from telling you more. Keep in mind that it is not a speechwriter's role, let alone his job description, to usurp authority; it's just that authority sometimes usurps you.

It is also not morally proper to be too self-deprecating. It is so easy in large organizations, especially in situations everyone knows are important, up to and including those with literally life-and-death consequences, to abdicate judgment and responsibility in the comforting assumption that someone else will make the tough calls. But someone else doesn't always make those calls. If you're there, and you believe you can make a positive difference, well, you do it. How will you know for sure when to step forward in this kind of situation and when not to? You won't know for sure. Sorry.

Recommended Reading

Pericles, "The Glory That Is Greece," in William Safire, ed., *Lend Me Your Ears: Great Speeches in History,* updated and expanded ed. (New York: W.W. Norton, 2004).

Winston Churchill's "Iron Curtain" speech at Westminster College, Fulton, MO, March 5, 1946, in William Safire, ed., *Lend Me Your Ears: Great Speeches in History,* updated and expanded ed. (New York: W.W. Norton, 2004).

Woodrow Wilson's Second Inaugural Address, 1917, in *Inaugural Addresses of the Presidents of the United States* (Washington, DC: GPO, 1989), www.bartleby.com/124/ (accessed January 10, 2012).

Secretary of State Condoleezza Rice's speech at the Institut d'Etudes Politiques de Paris, February 8, 2005, http://usa.usembassy.de/etexts/docs/riceparis020805e.htm (accessed January 10, 2012).

Matthew Scully, "Building a Better State of the Union Address," *New York Times,* February 2, 2005.

Peggy Noonan, *What I Saw at the Revolution: A Political Life in the Reagan Era* (New York: Random House, 1990), ch. 5.

John C. Kornblum, "Reagan's Brandenburg Concerto," *The American Interest,* May/June 2007.

Wynton Hall, "Reagan's Secret Formula," February 23, 2007, http://townhall.com/columnists/wyntonhall/2007/02/23/reagan%E2%80%99s_secret_formula.

Robert A. Lehrman, *The Political Speechwriter's Companion: A Guide for Writers and Speakers* (Washington, DC: CQ Press, 2009.)

Writing Exercise

Write the inaugural address for the next President of the United States, timed for about a 30-minute delivery, and print out the text as instructed in the chapter.

8 LETTERS, TOASTS, AND CEREMONIALS

Letters are the small arms of political writing, as opposed to the howitzers and fighter jets. They are certainly purposeful, but of all the forms of political writing we have covered so far, letters are unique in that they are, in their essence, one-to-one communications. As pieces of persuasive writing, they bypass the multiple-audience problems that afflict other types of political communication.

Indeed, there is only one form of writing that is even more circumscribed than letter writing, and that is diary writing: Voilà—where there were two, there is now only one. But political diaries are not meant to persuade, except ex post facto; political diary entries are meant to orient (or reorient) the writer in his own field of vision. It is the wise writer who realizes that to know what one thinks, one must first write it down; and so an author sometimes needs to externalize before he can analyze.

When I speak of letters, I mean real letters—not letters to the editor, which are really just short op-eds masquerading as letters. Nor do I mean "open letters," which amount to the same thing. I certainly don't mean chain letters, and if you doubt that you'll have bad luck for the next seven years.

Letters are purposeful in two ways. One of these ways is obvious, and of a kind with virtually all the forms of political language we have already discussed: to persuade. But there is another purpose to letters, too: They are among the forms of language that are ritualistic in character. *Letters bind.* Letters create stability in personal relations and develop those relations forward. Letters establish and maintain a bond of confidence among correspondents. Indeed, a correspondence can lie fallow for some time after it has been established, and the intimacy of it can be maintained for a long while if the letters that characterize the relationship are written skillfully and properly. But this latter capacity is really only possible when letter writing is transformed into a correspondence.

This is an important distinction. A letter, or a single exchange of letters, is just a letter or two; an ongoing discussion in writing that involves multiple exchanges over time is a correspondence. A correspondence has dimensions that mere exchanges of letters cannot have. Letters within a genuine correspondence, such as those written by Franklin Roosevelt and Winston Churchill during World War II, can refer back to exchanges not just before the last one, but to any one or many. Correspondences have depth; they accumulate reference points; they have texture.

That is why there is an entire genre of literature devoted to letters and correspondence. Much of this concerns the world of literature. Just as there are critics, and biographies of critics, and reviews of biographies of critics who are themselves reviewers of a sort, literature is a field that loves letters and correspondences. It may be unkind to point this out, but those who study and teach about fiction writing may not themselves be any good at it, so they write about personalities and their relationships instead.

In politics and public policy, we value the letters of famous people mainly for any new light they may cast on their authors' public personae. But the appetite for gossip is nearly universal, and most observers are also interested in personal matters and intimacies that have no real bearing on the public lives of famous people.[1]

What does the direct communication and intimacy of a letter allow that other kinds of political writing do not? First of all, they allow confidence itself. In a genuine letter, whether a formal political/diplomatic exchange or something else, we know that the material in a letter typically will not be shared. So one can say things one might otherwise not.

This is not an impermeable rule, however. Letters *are* sometimes shared, as Roosevelt shared one of Chiang Kai-shek's letters about India with Churchill.[2] Sometimes letters are even written knowing, suspecting, or *hoping* they might be shared, and that may well be the main purpose for writing the letter in the first place: communicating

---

1. See Joseph Epstein, *Gossip: The Untrivial Pursuit* (New York: Houghton Mifflin Harcourt, 2011), for a witty and penetrating analysis of this human foible.

2. "Roosevelt to Churchill for Chiang Kai-shek" and "Churchill's Reply," in Warren F. Kimball, ed., *Churchill & Roosevelt: The Complete Correspondence*, 3 vols. (Norwalk, CT: Easton Press, 1995).

something indirectly to a third party using the recipient of the letter merely as a witting or unwitting medium of transmission.

There are lots of examples in political history of such stratagems. Over the centuries, letters, full of lies, have been written about huge military movements and aggressive intentions, sent to damsels and vassals who promptly turned over or sold the information to intended targets, who were then made very afraid and who retreated or entreated the other party, all based on bluff and lying. This sounds very medieval, and it is; but it is also part of the contemporary intelligence operations trade as well. Such skullduggery is especially common in forms of industrial espionage and high finance, only nowadays e-mail instead of paper and ink is a more common means of communication.

All that said, if a long-term correspondence is at hand, both sides typically expect that what is said will be kept in confidence, and usually it is, at least until the death of one or both of the parties. At that point, letters are either destroyed or handed down to those who cannot know them perfectly, but who can know them nonetheless.[3] In political history, letters and especially correspondences are personal complements, along with diaries and memoirs, to archives.

It is the promise of confidentiality that allows a writer to personalize a message of persuasion—to use the known personal history of the recipient, for example, to deliver the point. A skilled letter writer knows how to create a proportion between the personal aspects of a message and the more general, substantive ones, and this knowledge depends on the writer's familiarity with the recipient. You really have to know the person you're writing to—again, know your audience, even if it is composed of just one person. But there almost always has to be some personal content as well, or the letter will seem stiff, stuffy, and out of frame for the purpose of persuasion.

To achieve its aim, a letter usually must have something to offer: a promise of support, perhaps, a pledge of new effort, or perhaps a piece of useful, marketable information. It is comparable to a deliverable in a speech, though it need not form the organizing principle of a letter. Very often in correspondence, as in commerce and as in life, one must give in order to receive.

When one is talking about letters between heads of state, say between

3. Good examples may be found in Cokie Roberts's book about the women of the founding generation, *Founding Mothers: The Women Who Raised Our Nation* (New York: HarperCollins, 2004).

President Harry Truman and the Iranian Prime Minister Mohammad Mossadegh, an exchange of letters is a bond so strong that it amounts to negotiation.[4] Positions may be established, advanced, and changed in letters; these letters then become, in diplomacy, official parts of the diplomatic record.

Letters, too, allow for genuine argument in a way that even personal conversations sometimes cannot.[5] Once something is committed to paper, it takes on a permanence that mere speech often does not impart. Letters also allow for the expression of personal emotion in the writer, as opposed to emotion anticipated in the reader, in a way that other forms of political writing do not. Letters are fully human, therefore, even when they are insincere; after all, insincerity is part of being human, too. As Marx once said, "Honesty and sincerity are the two most important human virtues; if you can fake those, you've got it made." (That's Groucho Marx, of course, not Karl.)

There are no hard-and-fast rules for general letter writing because the diversity of letters as to topic, personalities, and occasions is virtually infinite. And while letters always have some ritualistic element, as in the salutation and ending, they are never merely ritualistic or formal. Unless there is some kind of unanticipatable substance in a letter—the very opposite of the lexical content in a ritual in written form—it isn't really a letter at all.

There are six general rules of letter writing.

RULE 1: As already noted, there must be a calculated, deliberate balance between the personal and the substantive side of any letter.

RULE 2: In your letter (unlike in a formal essay), use "I" and "you." It has to be personal or the form is being either wasted or misused.

RULE 3: Don't mix too many—some say any—different topics or themes in a single letter. Better a short letter on a particular point, and

---

4. "Truman to Mossadegh," "Mossadegh to Truman," in *The Public Papers of the President: Harry S. Truman, 1951,* http://www.trumanlibrary.org/publicpapers/index.php (accessed January 15, 2012).

5. For a wonderful example from classical antiquity, see "Cicero to Cassius," in W. Glynn Williams, trans., *Cicero: Letters to His Friends,* Vol. 2: *Books VII–XII* (Cambridge, MA: Harvard University Press, 1928).

then another and another, than a long rambling letter that conflates many disparate topics. Such long and rambling letters represent an indulgence, and indulgences always have their eventual costs.

RULE 4: Craft your letter always to invite a response. A letter should never be closed-ended. All letter writing should aspire to turn into correspondence, in other words, for that is the apogee of the form.

RULE 5: Aesthetics are important, so consider carefully whether to use handwriting or typeface, stationery, stamps, and seals; all those kinds of considerations matter.

RULE 6: Think of a letter as a speech delivered, in writing, to one person.

Let me elaborate a bit on this final rule. If a letter can be conceived as a kind of performance, but for just one person, then like a speech it will work best when it tells some kind of story, and when you know well the audience to whom you are telling it. Just as in an oral presentation, you can use sentence fragments, repetition, and rhetorical questions—as long as you don't overdo it. You can and sometimes should enmesh a letter in a kind of sacred narrative, but one built up from personal knowledge of what matters to the recipient. A letter should be drafted with both purpose and message in mind. As with a speech, the structure of a letter should be clean and proportional to your purpose in writing it. Don't write five pages to get a small favor, or just a few lines requesting that someone risk his fortune or life.

Additionally, drawing once more on what we have already covered in discussing speechwriting and other forms of political persuasion, be mindful of an even tone, and avoid too much wit. It is fine to have a little fun and challenge the recipient to reciprocate, but one should not try to use a letter to create intimacy in a relationship where it does not already exist for some other reason. That makes a letter look forced and pretentious.

A letter, too, as with a speech, can be dramatic, even in the context of an ongoing correspondence. Here, too, you need to find the mean between clarity and unpredictability, between using the security vouchsafed by the correspondence and saying something truly new and different. In diplomacy, a two- or three-page letter can be significant for one sentence, or even just one phrase, that departs from past practice.

What is new can be modest and subtle, and more dramatic for so being in the context of a diplomatic correspondence (and here I use the word *diplomatic* both literally and figuratively). This corresponds, metaphorically at least, with the observation that one can often best see objects in the night sky using peripheral rather than direct vision. When you make someone search, or think, to find the payoff in a letter, you can sometimes raise the recipient's interest in the subject.

That, at least, used to be the case in the good ol' days. Now people talk on the phone more than write actual letters, and they e-mail and text with such abandon as to sometimes make telephone conversations seem quaint. In America and the West, if not also in much of the rest of the world, people are more informal in nearly every respect than they used to be. They often do not consider carefully exactly how to say what they want to say; what has gone out of style in personal life is frequently a wasting consideration in professional life, as well.

This informality carries certain risks beyond those inherent in imprecision. The reason is that some cultures, or at least some islands of professional discipline within some other cultures, still do take formal language very seriously, in business as well as in diplomacy. So, while in the United States and still a bit less so in Europe political communication is often undertaken in a rather informal, matter-of-fact way, in East Asia—China especially, but also Japan and Korea—analysts pour over every word, every comma, comparing it assiduously to previous communications on the same topic. Here we have two cultures with vastly different traditions of letter writing and language usage, and it creates some interesting challenges.

In April 2001 a serious incident occurred involving the United States and China. It is known in the literature as the EP-3 incident. An intelligence-gathering aircraft of that description, clearly marked as a U.S. Air Force plane, was flying in international waters off China's southeastern coast when a Chinese fighter pilot tried to force the plane down. In the ensuing aerial dynamics, the fighter-plane pilot damaged his craft and his plane crashed, killing him. The U.S. plane was also damaged and set down on Hainan Island. The Chinese government blamed the United States for the incident, and for the death of its pilot. The U.S. government, very justifiably, saw things differently: The U.S. reconnaissance plane, being in international airspace, was not at fault. It took several days for the United States to get its crew, and eventually its plane, back. The Chinese government insisted on a public apology from the United States, but the United States was very reluctant to apologize for something that was not its fault. Eventually, language was worked out that the Chinese could interpret as an apology, and that the U.S. government could interpret as something less than that. Of course, these messages and statements had to be translated back and forth from English to Chinese and from Chinese to English. Languages from different language families rarely translate simply or directly. That creates a problem in letter writing among individuals from different languages, but it also enables diplomats to take advantage of the inherent ambiguities of translations to solve disagreements. In this case and no doubt in many others, ambiguity became a blessing.

It is probably worth taking just a moment to describe another matter, also bearing on letters and translations, this one in which I had some personal involvement. In the first few years of the George W. Bush administration, U.S. relations with Russia had become peppered with suspicion and difficulty. Still, the public face of U.S. rhetoric remained placid and utterly without rancor. In the months and years following 9/11, pressure continued to build within the United States against Russia. Many observers believed the Bush administration was closing its eyes to Russia's dismal record on human rights and to the security of new allies, all in order to win Moscow's cooperation on antiterrorism matters.

In January 2004, Secretary of State Powell visited Moscow. He and his senior administration colleagues decided that along with the private, confidential messages he brought to the Russian leadership, including a personal letter from President Bush to Vladimir Putin, he would make a public statement as well. That public statement, designed in part to placate U.S. domestic opinion but also to toughen policy toward Russia in a subtle but unmistakable fashion, took the form of an op-ed, or open letter, to the Russian people published on the front page of the newspaper *Izvestia*. It was my job, along with colleagues who were expert in Russian language, society, and politics, to write that open letter.

As these things go, the assignment was a rush job. I did my best, and then we entered into a sensitive process of translation that required native speakers to examine every paragraph, every sentence, every word, and the interactions of all three. I do not read or understand Russian, but I did know which single, subtle, but unmistakable sentence represented the business end in this piece of writing. Between staff at what is called Main State, at 22nd and C Streets in Washington—also known as Foggy Bottom—and staff at Embassy Moscow, we literally spent hours, many of them on just one sentence, making sure that what the Secretary wanted to convey worked in translation. It did, and the public communication worked to create a useful context for the private communications the Secretary brought with him.

The lesson for you? In the real world of politics, whether international diplomacy or domestic politics, different forms of persuasive language invariably combine to create an overall impression. Speeches, letters, op-eds, essays, and all the rest come together to form an overarching communications environment. Each piece works in relationship to the others. The idea is that whole should be designed to produce more deliberate persuasive impact than the sum of the parts, not less. Alas, the latter is a more common outcome. If you seek illustrative examples, write me a letter asking for them. Perhaps we will develop a correspondence.

With letters now understood better, let us move on to toasts, thank-you notes, and other ceremonials. Before getting to specific how-to language, however, we again need to take a brief step back to understand something about the nature of all these forms of persuasive writing.

Most of you will have heard the phrase—from a 1954 hit song by Kitty Kallen—that "little things mean a lot." Song lyric or no, it's true. Toasts, award presentations, thank-yous, and condolence notes are all little things. They are composed of just a few sentences sometimes; at most they amount to short speeches or letters. But they *do* mean a lot, and they require skill sets and sensibilities that go beyond those needed for an op-ed, an essay, a standard speech, and so forth. Indeed, because they are so short, they are often much more difficult to craft well than longer kinds of writing. They represent extreme cases of "less is more." Every word must not only "carry water," it must shine your shoes, brush your teeth, and tell you how good-looking you are, as well.

Now, you may think that writing such little items represents an exception to the rule, to the first commandment of all political language: Thou shalt persuade. But it is not an exception. With such little writings, you *are* indeed trying to persuade others, but you are not trying to persuade with an argument, and you are usually not trying to persuade on matters of substance. What you are doing is persuading someone that you care; that you are refined and of good character; that you respect tradition; that you are civilized within the special and specific realm of the political and/or diplomatic profession, or within whatever professional or familial subculture you are enmeshed.

And make no mistake: Every profession has its subculture. Every profession is in some ways still a guild: Access is marketed, and unde-sirables are kept out. This is done by establishing framework conven-tions, and teaching acolytes how to operate within them. So the ability to write these little kinds of items is a way into a professional and subcultural domain. It is your union card, so to speak. If you can't do these things, you can't get in, and if you can't get in, you can't persuade anyone about anything.

This is what Groucho was on to: People fake sincerity all the time, and people know that others are faking. But it's a ritual, and these things need to be done properly. Properly constructed insincerity within a ritual format allows us to get along. It lets us put away the natural rough edges in relationships that are professional but not always personal. It bears to some degree on the concept of politeness, a word everyone has heard but that few have ever actually thought about. Is politeness a means to create intimacy, or is it the reverse, a way to keep other people at arm's length? In truth, it is both, and neither. Politeness is a modulator, a balancer, between the two, and by so being it allows for civility where there is neither intimacy nor alienation. When a public official writes a condolence letter or gives an award, everyone knows that a lot of time he doesn't give a proverbial rat's ass about the award or about the person or persons to whom it is being given. But to give the impression that he does is a skill having everything to do with polite-ness, and that skill is necessary to many kinds of jobs. At some level, probably, it is necessary to every job, save for those that are completely solipsistic (if you don't know this word, do not skip it lazily; stop and look it up, as I instructed you to do several chapters ago). Hypocrisy must wrap itself into an art form in order to become a civilizing force (you should have taken time to read the Alan Ehrenhalt op-ed cited in Chapter 6). Otherwise, it's just bad faith and bad behavior.

Finally, before getting down to specifics, note something that is critically common to all these forms. Whether it's a toast, an award, a thank-you note, or a memorial of some kind, all of these forms involve a twin specialty: A person or persons are being singled out; an event, act, or occasion is being singled out; and the two are always paired. For a toast, there is the person being toasted and there is the occasion of the toast. For a thank-you note, you are thanking a specific person or persons for some specific act. For a condolence letter, you are focused *not* on who has died—death is the event; the special person is rather the one who is bereaved. For an award, of course, it's the awardee and the reason for the award.

Now, this observation, as embarrassingly simple as it is, gives away the basic rule of how to write all forms of this sort: Emphasize the special person and the special event or act or occasion, and link them together. Everything else is extraneous. Everything else, except for purposes of preparing the way for the delivery of the key message, should belong among your principles of exclusion for this kind of writing job.

And here is another never-fail piece of advice that applies to all of these kinds of things: Don't go over the top. Sincerity and overdoing it are nonfitting parts; they are mutually exclusive. Genuine sincerity is always understated. So if you want to successfully fake sincerity, don't be excessive about it.

Let's start with the particularities of thank-you notes. Whether you are drafting language for yourself or someone else—it doesn't matter—a thank-you note has five parts. So there are five rules, or better in this case steps, for writing them.

STEP 1: Get the name and address and salutation exactly right. No misspellings are tolerable. Check, recheck, and check again, because screwing up a salutation is even worse—because more personal—than mispronouncing someone's name in the grace notes of a speech. Sincerity goes right down the toilet when you communicate that you don't care enough to really know to whom it is you are writing.

STEP 2: Make your first sentence specific and concrete: "Thank you for the lovely" whatever. State not just the gift, but also the place or time or occasion of its giving. Paint a little picture of the gifting. Fashion a small story that works to recreate the emotion of the moment; that is your way to building a bridge between the event warranting the thank-you note and the recipient's reading of it. Be brief.

STEP 3: In your second sentence, generalize. Once you have concretized the gifting, generalize about the relationship that led to the gifting. You might write something like, "My gratitude is emblematic of our sincere friendship, one that has stood the test of time and has served us all well." The situation will provide any proper nouns you will need to make this generalization work for you.

STEP 4: In your next sentence speak of the future. Indicate, in other words, that the relationship that led to the gifting is ongoing.

STEP 5: Reconcretize and close. Mention, if possible, some work or some interest in common, as specific as possible, and then get off the stage. If you have written more than seven or eight sentences, your note is too long. If you have written fewer than five, it is too short.

That's it. This isn't rocket science. Not every situation will be applicable to this formula, but most will.

You must also, of course, pay attention to aesthetics, as is the case with letters of all kinds. In many circumstances, handwriting is better than type. But for formal matters, type is fine, although not a sans-serif type of the kind you would use to create a speech text. (But don't choose a cursive one, either; that's overboard.) Don't use legal-size stationery, or stark raving white stationery. Use cream, and smaller paper and envelope. Stagger your addresses, unlike in a business correspondence, and always use stamps, never a postal meter.

In general, too, if you want mail to get noticed and be received as a personal statement, stick with stamps. Even people who never think about these kinds of things subliminally know the difference between the impersonal and the personal. Metered mail is like bulk mail, impersonal to the bone. Stamps, the more aesthetic the better, convey just the opposite impression.

With awards ceremonial presentations, there are six rules or steps to follow.

STEP 1: Don't lunge. Set up the event and draw people in. "Welcome to [whatever, wherever] on this beautiful [winter/spring] [day/evening/afternoon], where we will join together to [whatever it is]."

Why do this? Because, if you are wise, you know that you need to create an instant community of the moment. Always use "we," never "I" to start, unless you are a major public figure, and even then "I" is worth avoiding.

STEP 2: Tell a story about the awardee. Having concretized the moment, now humanize the award.

STEP 3: Now go back and describe the origins and purpose of the award.

STEP 4: Explain why awardee fits the award and deserves it. In other words, work on your obligatory pairing of person and occasion.

STEP 5: Enact the dramatic climax: Literally bestow the award. It might be a piece of paper, like an honorary degree. Sometimes it will be framed. Sometimes the award will be a trophy of some sort. Often, actually, it will be some strange crystallized figurine that bears little resemblance to the act it commemorates.

Now, please take this next piece of advice seriously: Try to get the person who is to bestow the award a chance to handle the "thing" that is the award before the ceremony starts. Get a feel, or better have your principal, if you are writing for someone else, get a feel for the thing—how heavy it is, if it is awkward to handle in any way, or not easily set down without mishap. Once you are confident that the presenter will not drop the "thing," you must think of it as a baton that needs to be passed in a relay race. If you have training in track, you know that the key to passing a baton while on the hoof is to "look" the baton into the hand of the person to whom you are giving it. Same thing here: Awardees can be excited and distracted by a ceremony. They are apt to drop things; I have seen it happen. It is bad when that happens, so don't let it happen. Regard the "thing," the award, defensively.

STEP 6: Dance your denouement by talking about the future, about the awardee as a role model to others, or about common purposes or whatever is appropriate to the award. The point, again, is to use language to join the audience with the awardee and the purpose of the award into a community of the moment. Then get off the stage, or get to the side of it if, as usual, it is the awardee's turn to speak after you.

Again, this is not rocket science. It is common sense mostly, but as Voltaire, the genius of the Enlightenment, once quipped, "Common sense is not so common."

Next we come to the toast, which is probably the most misunderstood and roundly abused of all the forms discussed in this chapter. A toast is best thought of as a short poem. It needs meter, repetition, and lilt, and it can stand alliteration and occasional archaisms like "'tis" and "to wit" and so on. But above all, it has to connect the person toasted with the occasion for the toast.

Some basic rules of thumb that work for thank-you notes also work for toasts. Again, it's always "we," not "I" unless the "I" is the President of the United States or the Secretary of State, and even then.... A toast works, nearly always, as a concise, slowly spoken, five-part exercise. So here we go again: Prepare yourself to learn and practice five steps.

STEP 1: Stand and address the object of the toast, generally with toastee's name with full title, that person's entourage, followed by "ladies and gentlemen." So you might say, "To Congressman Dewey Cheatum, of the great state of [whatever], Mrs. Cheatum, the [whatever] delegation, ladies and gentlemen."

STEP 2: Say: "We are honored" and then fill in why. You must do this within a single sentence.

STEP 3: Say: "We are reminded" and then fill in something that crystallizes the significance of the occasion. This must also be done, if possible, within a single sentence. Do not babble, or have the principal for whom you are writing babble.

STEP 4: Say: "We look forward to" and fill in something that makes sense but is not too specific—because that breaks the magical spell with the quotidian. Do this also in a single sentence if you possibly can.

STEP 5: Finally, say: "Raise your glasses, everyone please, and let us say," and then you pick one or at most two words. That can be "welcome" or "farewell" or "to peace" or "to victory" or "to friendship" or, at most, "thank you, sir." But again, do not babble. Just smile more or less broadly, make eye contact with the guest of honor as you do, take a sip and *sit down*. Let people get to their booze, broth, and beefsteak.

Now, this formula will not be appropriate for every imaginable occasion at which a toast might be offered. For all I know, it's an absolutely a terrible way to proceed if you are the best man standing to hold forth at a wedding rehearsal dinner in Jodhpor, India. But for most purposes, this formula will at least get you started and keep you—or your principal—safe from embarrassment.

The most common reason by far for the making of very bad toasts, aside from preprandial inebriation, is the simple fact that most people don't realize what they are doing. Toasts are poems, not speeches, not proclamations, not the pouring out of one's inner soul, not an occasion for telling a joke, or anything else. When people do not know what they are doing, their natural anxiety tends to open up their mouths as they hunt around for what they dimly imagine a toast should accomplish.[6] Most of the time, too, they speak much too fast, a phenomenon also associated with general anxiety. By the time they finish hunting, there is still most often no actual toast in sight, but a great deal has been blathered about, most of it usually undecipherable.

If you have ever witnessed such a scene, or if you have been responsible for one yourself—heaven forbid—then you realize full well that this is a situation definitely to be avoided. So even if my little five-step formula for toasts does not strike the right note for all occasions, it works at the very least as a guarantee against unmitigated disasters of the babbling kind.

Speaking of disaster and other kinds of sadness, let us now take up the crafting of condolence letters. There are six steps to writing these, too, and in this case the order is important to the point of critical.

STEP 1: Get right to the point: "Please accept my condolence over the loss of—or sometimes, better, 'the passing of'—[so-and so], your [name the relationship]."

STEP 2: Praise the deceased, and triangulate if at all possible: In other words, get the three of you—deceased, addressee, and you the writer—together again in recollection if you were ever together in fact. This helps to concretize the message.

STEP 3: Empathize with their pain. Choose your words very carefully as appropriate to the specific situation.

STEP 4: Offer comfort and hope, again as appropriate to the specific case. Be personal; use names and lots of future tense.

STEP 5: Concretize again, looking to the future: "If there is anything I can do, . . ." and try if you can to find a parting metaphor that symbolizes the personality, image, profession, something about the deceased. But use only one metaphor.

---

6. Anyone can screw up a toast. For one example, see "Toasts of the President and the President of Ecuador," June 22, 1951, from *The Public Papers of the President: Harry S. Truman, 1951*. Both toasts recorded here in the official record are bloody awful.

I once drafted a condolence letter for Secretary Powell on the passing of the former Chairman of the Joint Chiefs of Staff, Admiral Thomas Moorer. The letter was to his widow, and it ended, "May fair skies and a following wind comfort you in your sweet memories," or something like that. Navy talk, you know. That's what the situation suggested. In all probability, it worked.

STEP 6: It is very good, if you can pull it off, to move from short choppy sentences in the beginning of such a note to longer and more graceful, lyrical sentences toward the end. Here is why: Most people, when they are grieving, are often short of speech and of breath. That's what crying, or being on the verge of tears, does to human speech patterns. So the very design of your letter should bring comfort: It should carry the reader from an initial jolt, for you in this note are inevitably reminding them of something very painful, to a more relaxed, full-breathing, consoling conclusion.

Now, let us end, appropriately I think, with memorials. Memorials of all kinds are essentially religious texts. If they have to do with death, they are necessarily religious in character because dealing with death, after all, is one of the reasons religion is universally invented and used. Therefore, the key to success here is to find some way to ascribe purpose to the lives of those deceased.

A memorial is also a usually speech. It is meant mainly to be heard, not read—although there are exceptions.[7] Therefore, a memorial presentation generally follows the rules for all speeches. It needs a simple

---

7. I once wrote a memorial speech for Secretary Powell after the Foreign Minister of Sweden, Anna Lindh, was knifed to death by a lunatic in Stockholm. The speech was meant to be read at a memorial service in Stockholm, but the Secretary's plane could not get off the ground due to a hurricane. So at the last minute the text was sent to the U.S. Ambassador to Sweden for him to read at the memorial service, a turn of events of the kind that gives speechwriters nightmares. I had never met this man; I had no idea if a speech I had crafted for Powell, who knew Anna Lindh well, would work for him, or would instead have him say things that would sound off-key or be plainly inappropriate. In addition, the speech was translated into Swedish and published the next day in virtually every Swedish daily newspaper. But what I wrote was a text in English for a performance art, not something to be turned into translated ink. Some of my non-speechwriting associates at the State Department failed to appreciate the reason for my anxiety over all this. As it happened, everything turned out fine; no one was embarrassed and the language did its job.

structure. It needs repetition to organize what is being said for the listener. Beyond that, following these six rules, or rather pieces of advice in this case, will help.

RULE 1: Speak more slowly than you usually do. Rushing through a memorial presentation sends all the wrong signals. If you have to, speckle a text with directional asides for the speaker to slow down. Speaking slowly, and softly as well, connotes reverence, humility, and a contemplative mood, all of which are appropriate for such occasions. Rapid speech often connotes levity, egoism, and impatience—that's bad, very bad, for occasions like these.

RULE 2: The posing and answering of questions is a good device in memorial presentations. The use of rhetorical questions as a literary device works only occasionally in a speech, but it seems a better fit in a memorial, possibly because death by its very nature evokes more questions than it ever does answers. The use of rhetorical questions works to draw the audience in; it affirms the mystery of birth and death not far from everyone's inner consciousness on such occasions; it helps make that instant community these ritual occasions need.

RULE 3: Use one or at most two quotations from appropriate sources to produce instant transcendence. The text must be from sacred writ, but that can be so either literally or secularly. Avoid quotes that may be even the slightest bit controversial or that might split the room into factions. Any quotation you use must be unifying in its impact but also possess meaning that stands clear on its own. If you have to stop and explain what a quotation means, it is the wrong choice.

RULE 4: Use a touch of lightening humor, but be *exceedingly* careful as to how you go about it. People want to be comforted. They want the mood to be something other than wholly gloomy. They are looking for inspiration and hope, or at any rate are glad to accept it if it finds them. You can sometimes get from grief to hope through the bridge of humor, but humor that makes use of humility on the part of the speaker.

RULE 5: Try to use the condolence-letter technique of beginning with short choppy sentences opening out into longer and more rhythmic ones. Indeed, this method works even better at a spoken-word event than it does in a letter of condolence.

RULE 6: Don't cry. You can choke up a little, and be halting. You can even pause and dip your chin. But you should not cry if you can help it, because that is over the top. It may be viewed as stealing unless you can honestly say that you knew the deceased better than anyone, or at least very well. To cry for others, and to break the mood down that way at such a sensitive time, robs them of their right to cry for themselves.

As I say, sometimes this is not a matter of choice. But since it is on balance not a good idea to cry, you can steel yourself not to do so. And the way you do that is to make very sure you have practiced delivering a text, even if you (or your principal, if you are writing for someone else) decide in the moment not to rely directly on it. Having a text forces you to anticipate the emotional pressure of the moment, at least to some extent. As you draft and practice that text, you project yourself into the moment of its delivery. That helps you keep control of your emotions when that moment arrives.

More than once I have seen a very practiced speaker go into a memorial ceremony determined to speak straight from the heart only to lose control and make a real hash out of the occasion, to their subsequent deep regret. Don't let this happen to you, or to someone who is relying on you. It is one thing to screw up a toast. Most people soon get into their cups and forget all about it. But if you screw up a memorial presentation, the memory of it has a tendency to linger long after everyone has gone home. You don't get a second chance at these things.

Recommended Reading

"Cicero to Cassius," in W. Glynn Williams, trans., *Cicero: Letters to His Friends,* Vol. 2: *Books VII–XII* (Cambridge, MA: Harvard University Press, 1928).

"Roosevelt to Churchill for Chiang Kai-shek" and "Churchill's Reply," in Warren F. Kimball, ed., *Churchill & Roosevelt: The Complete Correspondence,* 3 vols. (Norwalk, CT: Easton Press. 1995), vol. 1.

"Truman to Mossadegh," "Mossadegh to Truman," in *The Public Papers of the President: Harry S. Truman, 1951,* http://www.trumanlibrary.org/publicpapers/index.php (accessed January 15, 2012).

"Toasts of the President and the President of Ecuador," June 22, 1951, from *The Public Papers of the President: Harry S. Truman, 1951.*

Writing Exercise

Write a letter to a graduate school admissions office, asking to be admitted to a program of your desire. Then write a toast to your mother, in the voice of your father, on the occasion of your own birth.

9 MEMORANDA

A memorandum is the main means of formal substantive communication in any bureaucracy, including all political bureaucracies. The entire persuasive art form is indecipherable and indescribable except in the context of the hierarchies that inhere in bureaucracies and organizations of all kinds. Genuine memos never stay on the same rung of the bureaucratic ladder (with one special exception I'll mention in a moment); they always go either up or down in that hierarchy. There is no need to write a memo to someone who is your equal in an organization: You just talk to that person, or you brainstorm and think out loud with your colleagues. That kind of creative interchange usually should not be on paper anyway. If those who are formally at the same level of an organization are writing memos to each other, then one is implicitly senior to the other for some reason or the collegial relationship leaves much to be desired.

Memos are about position and power. They are vehicles of persuasion par excellence. They are written as much or more to offices and functions of a bureaucracy as they are to actual flesh-and-blood human beings. Memos meant to persuade and exert influence in a hierarchy can have three main purposes: to generate actionable ideas; to form coalitions to support or oppose actionable ideas; and to assert management and/or budgetary control over others. The most effective memos, from a strictly organizational point of view, do all three at the same time.

Of course, not all memoranda are action memoranda. Some memoranda merely announce to a superior or a subordinate that one is still breathing and reasonably sentient. Another purpose for a memo is to establish a paper trail for legal or administrative reasons, like stating when you'll be on vacation, how you want your pension invested, and other matters of like and "lite" sort. But these are not real memos, not "action memoranda." They are merely process memos of one sort or another.

Some memos—rather a lot in government, to be truthful—look like action memos but really are not. These are memos that are written mainly to protect the posterior of the writer from future troubles. Many are created to dissociate the author from some impending action from which she dissents, which is why Dean Acheson, the U.S. Secretary of State from 1949 to 1953, is reputed to have said that "a memorandum is written not to inform the reader but to protect the writer."

Now, whatever its purpose, how do you write one of these things? As with all other forms of persuasive writing, you can get a good impression of high and lesser quality by reading examples. The more examples you read, the better you will appreciate the diversity and the skills of the memorandum art. Unfortunately, by their very nature, memoranda are meant to stay within the walls of an organization. Memoranda bear several similarities to op-eds, as we shall see, but they are the complete opposite of op-eds in that the latter is meant to be maximally public, while the former is meant to be maximally private.

Whatever is intended for memoranda when they are written, they do have a tendency to leak into the public domain from time to time. In the world of diplomacy, the record, called *The Foreign Relations of the United States*, or the *FRUS* for short, is available virtually by the ton; within it are tens of thousands of historical memoranda for your review. Or you can simply retrieve the WikiLeaks trove of 2011 to see what recent memos look like.

If you read or generate enough of these, you'll appreciate that, the challenges of their diversity notwithstanding, there are three general memo-writing rules one can know and follow.

First, keep it short, and keep the sentences and paragraphs within it short. Rhetorical flourishes, asides, footnotes, quotes (except from the very highest source), jokes, witticisms, aphorisms—forget it. These are all out of place in a memo. This is the main thing that distinguishes a memo from an op-ed. In length and general purpose, they may be the same, but they are totally different in tone. An op-ed must dazzle and entertain, as well as be cogent, to do its job. A memo must be serious in the extreme: It must be relentlessly precise and never flowery.

Moreover, the higher you are reaching up an organization's chain of command, the shorter and more serious your memo should be. If you are communicating to an immediate superior, you can prattle on some, because you know the material is going to be reshaped before it reaches the actual decision maker. But if you're writing for the decision maker himself, keep it very short.

Why care so much about length? The reason is that your superiors either really are busy persons or they like others to think they are; so don't waste their time. That's the number one and most obvious reason. But more important than that, senior decision makers in any bureaucracy know that if someone cannot write concisely and persuasively, then they do not yet really know what they are talking about. If you cannot express the essence of your idea and purpose in one uncomplicated sentence, then your idea is not yet ready for prime time. And if you go prematurely and long, you have already devalued yourself in the eyes of that superior. Oh, beware the shot from the hip that boomerangs and strikes the author in the rear. Woe betide the impetuous memorandumist.

This warning brings us back to the importance of developing internal standards of excellence. If you have to write 10 drafts of an essay or a review or an op-ed before you are satisfied that it is really done, the same goes for a memo. Just because it is an internal document does not mean that its capacity to persuade can be achieved with less relative effort.

Second, or perhaps first in many situations, decide your addressee or addressees. This may sound a little silly to you, but it's not. Indeed, the first thing you need to do is to define who "you" are. It is not always self-evident that only one person should sign an action memo. Sometimes memoranda accumulate in chains of association. One person may have an idea but conclude that the idea would have a better chance of moving forward if other people joined in signing it. Oftentimes in government, it ultimately takes a posse to move an idea forward, and that posse needs to be composed of individuals strategically placed in the decision process. Sometimes an initial memo will get elevated as its proposal matures, and its signatories may change as it does. It is a good idea for the person who first has the idea to be able to anticipate as much as possible this kind of process. That comes from experience and from knowing one's organizational environment.

Only after you have decided who should sign a memorandum can you begin the process of figuring out to whom it should be addressed. Should you choose your immediate superior? Usually you should, or you risk irritating that person for going out of channel, out of line, or over their head. But there are cases where the risk-averse nature of bureaucracies is such that an idea sent to an immediate supervisor can be harmful to you. It can imply, in effect, "Hey boss, why didn't you think of this?" It can tag a person as an upstart or troublemaker. These are very real considerations in many large organizations, not to exclude the Pentagon, the White House, or even a large committee staff in Congress.

One reason for addressing your immediate superior *most* of the time is that the idea is more important than you are. As Ronald Reagan was fond of saying, "There is no limit to what you can accomplish if you don't care who gets the credit."[1] The most effective memo is one that makes the recipient think the idea was really his own. For example, "As you said last week, Mortimer, blah and blah and blah, and this suggests, does it not Mortimer, sir, that we should maximize the power of your insight by doing x, y, and q-squared."

You get it? You will get it or you won't get very far, because this sort of thing will get you farther faster in a career than trying to leapfrog your boss. You do best in a large organization when you achieve two things simultaneously: You become indispensable, and you are not a threat to the status of others. Memo wisdom can help you do this.

But in truth, the immediate superior is *not always* the right addressee for a memo. Sometimes, the immediate superior will be your main problem, your obstacle. The way you overcome such obstacles is not the Army way (pushing straight through it) but the Navy way (outflanking and maneuvering around it to set up a maximally opportune shot at the broadside of a target). The question is, how do you write an action memo to someone who isn't your immediate supervisor?

There are (at least) three ways to do this. One is to credit your boss with the idea in the memo and then copy him in (using CC:). A second is to ready the excuse that you didn't think the subject of the memo was important enough to bother the boss, but it seemed to fit into an area of special interest to so-and-so. This is disingenuous most of the time, and it's risky; but it sometimes works. And third is what we call the "up and over," or merely "over," option.

As noted earlier, there's only one exception to the rule that you never write a memo to someone who is your equal: If a bureaucracy is large enough, it may consist of segmented but parallel elements. One can

---

1. See http://books.google.com/books/about/Ronald_Reagan.html/?id=L-Oup8TM63MC.

refer to the State Department as a bureaucracy, for example. One can also refer to the National Security Council as a bureaucracy, albeit a smaller one. But one can rightfully describe both of these organizations and several others besides as being part of one larger bureaucracy, that of the U.S. government's foreign and national security policy apparatus. Put differently, different pieces of a large bureaucracy, which are bureaucracies themselves, can be thought of as functionally integrated in different ways.

Therefore, equals in rank in these departments can and do send action memos across agency divides. The same thing, presumably, can happen among congressional staffs and committees and in corporate environments. When doing this, a memo writer can sometimes go across and a little up. It helps a lot if the addressee of your memo is on more or less close personal terms with you. Informal networks are extremely important at these levels (and every level).[2] If your immediate superior knows that you know so-and-so at another agency—or to translate into the congressional vernacular, at another committee or subcommittee—she is less likely to be offended by a cross step. Or not; it depends on the situation. As in most cases in life, there is no substitute ultimately for situational awareness, prudential judgment, and emotional intelligence.

So to repeat: Know your addressee. The point, again, is to influence the decision maker, and unless you *are* the decision maker, this can only be done by indirection. The path matters, and the path you choose by deciding the addressee is the one the memo takes.

Also keep in mind that the size of the idea matters. You have to make a logical connection between the nature of the actionable idea you are proposing and what the addressee of your memo can possibly be expected to do about it. If your idea is too big, you will frustrate and irritate your reader(s), and open yourself to charges that you are an impractical dreamer. If your idea is too small, you will frustrate and irritate your readers, too, and open yourself to charges that you have no imagination. It's another of those pesky Goldilocks problems that we continue to encounter.

---

2. For an illuminating discussion of how informal networks operate at high levels of government, see the early chapters of Dov Zakheim, *A Vulcan's Tale: How the Bush Administration Mismanaged the Reconstruction of Afghanistan* (Washington, DC: Brookings Institution Press, 2011). Zakheim served as Pentagon Comptroller during the first George W. Bush administration, a position with the rank of Undersecretary. He was an original member of the famed, or infamous, Vulcans.

But what actual form does a memo take? In terms of format, there is no standard way to proceed. Follow the protocols of the subculture in which your organization resides. But format is less important than structure, and you should not confuse the two. Here is a 10-step formula, in sequence, that will rarely fail you.

STEP 1: Craft a hook. A memo, like an op-ed, should have an opening that grabs attention and leads into something the reader is likely already thinking about.

STEP 2: State the essence of the problem, and the essence of the proposed action recommended (either a solution or an objective). Note that in a memo you can almost always assume a lot more on the part of the reader than you can in an op-ed, so this helps you to be brief.

STEP 3: Then break a subhead and be very careful what you call it. A subhead is an opportunity to make a memorable point. The subhead should lead into the body of your case, where you lay out the problem in more detail and then describe the action you recommend to deal with it.

STEP 4: Make sure the action you are recommending is easily comprehensible, detailed enough to show you have thought it through, but not so down in the weeds that the memo loses energy, and hence the attention and hoped for enthusiasm of the reader. Use bullets and other devices if you wish to make sure your sketch is clean and clear, but don't overdo it. Don't turn a memo in a PowerPoint presentation without coherent English sentences.

STEP 5: Name the other actors who must be involved for this idea to work; rarely can any one office or agency get anything significant done by itself.

STEP 6: State the budgetary consequences, if any. This is more important these days than ever before.

STEP 7: Make explicit the phasing of a proposed action. If you don't break down the implementation of your idea into plausible parts, a reader may think it impractical or infeasible.

STEP 8: If possible, define with real metrics how to measure the progress of implementation. Decision makers are reluctant much of the time to spend political capital and take chances on behalf of hard-to-define or hard-to-measure aspirations. If you can concretize the expected dividends from a given course of action, you will make the adoption of that course more likely.

STEP 9: Anticipate obstacles, and assay ways to overcome them.

STEP 10: Restate in your conclusion (which of course you will not be so daft as to call a conclusion) the importance of the problem and the redeeming promise of the proposed action. It is almost always safe, and effective, to say that there is no stable status quo, and so that in the absence of action the problem will worsen. This statement has the ancillary merit of usually being true, so there is no need to be shy about it.

And that, dear reader, is the way to write a memo, win friends, and influence people.

Recommended Reading

S/P Memo (Dept. of State), W.W. Rostow to Dean Rusk, "Victory and Defeat in Guerilla Wars," May 20, 1965, in *The Pentagon Papers,* vol. 3 (Boston, MA: Beacon Press, 1971), ch. 3.

"Z. Brzezinski's Memo to President Carter, May 1, 1980," in *Zbigniew Brzezinski, Power and Principle: Memoirs of the National Security Adviser, 1977–1981* (New York: Farrar, Straus and Giroux, 1983).

"Donald Rumsfeld's Memo to Myers, Wolfowitz, Pace, and Feith," October 16, 2003, http://www.usatoday.com/news/washington/executive/rumsfeld-memo. htm (accessed January 15, 2012).

Todd Stern & William Antholis, "Toolbox," *The American Interest*, January/ February 2007.

Writing Exercise

Take the op-ed you wrote a little while ago and transform it into a memo. Take care to decide who should sign the memo and who its addressees should be.

10 COMMISSION REPORTS

Bill Cosby once began a comedy routine with the question, "Why is there air?" One might as well ask, "Why are there federal commissions?" The answer, however instructive, turns out not to be as funny.

There are federal commissions for some combination of three basic reasons. Some of these reasons may strike you as less noble than others, and that's because they are.

First, in recent years commissions have sometimes been created in order to manufacture jobs for retired or defeated prominenti and politicians. When that is a main reason for its creation, the commission in question is likely devoted to a problem that no one intends ever to seriously address. We witnessed a large expansion of showcase, make-work commissions during the eight years of Clinton presidency. Not only did that administration manage to balance the budget, it also excelled at producing sinecures for the tired, the well connected, and the underemployed.

A second and far more important reason for federal commissions is the need to deal with some rather serious problems that are not easily handled within the structure of the national government. This may be because of bureaucratic ineptitude, conflict, or lack of imagination. Sometimes, indeed, a certain bureaucracy or group of bureaucracies may *be* the problem, at least when commissions concern themselves, as they should, with the intersection of policy and governmental design. The government may also be ineffective because of excessive political partisanship; commissions offer a way to bracket, if not eliminate, political intrusions into efforts at problem solving. This is why commission reports often need to be written with understated tact and extreme care.[1]

---

1. See this example, which is attuned to the intelligence community: Mark M. Lowenthal, "Between the Lines of the Iraq Intelligence Estimate," *Washington Post*, February 11, 2007.

A third reason for federal commissions is that, depending on their sponsorship and what the sponsors mean to do with their work once the commission has finished with it, they can create political leverage for change by focusing high-level attention and status on an issue. At the same time, a commission can overcome partisanship in the way sponsorship and commission membership is arranged. Sometimes the prestige of members can accomplish this; other times the diversity of sponsorship accomplishes it. But sometimes there is conflicting sponsorship of commission reports on the same issue. This was the case in the aftermath of Hurricane Katrina, when both the White House and the Congress created commissions, both of which issued an extensive report on the disaster. When this happen, commissions become something akin to weapons in partisan or intergovernmental warfare.

There have been many important and consequential federal commissions in U.S. history. You have probably never heard of most of them, but some may sound familiar: the Warren Commission, which investigated the assassination of President John F. Kennedy; the Kerner Commission, on the 1968 urban riots; the 9/11 Commission; and more recently, if you have been following the news, the Simpson-Bowles Commission, which, had the President stood behind his own creation might have avoided the disastrous spectacle the American political system displayed to the world over the federal debt and debt ceiling in the summer of 2011.

Federal commissions are a relatively recent phenomenon. The old-fashioned way to tackle special projects outside established governmental channels was simply for the President or some important group of principals to call in friends and experts from the outside and informally get their counsel, and sometimes their help. This method was called into play, for example, when President Wilson decided to segregate government buildings in Washington, DC, in 1913. More or less the same thing happened when the government prevailed upon an American banker named Charles G. Dawes to advise it and then to implement wisely the reparations provisions of the Versailles Treaty.

Whatever else it did, the spirit of the Progressive movement had the effect of formalizing advice to government, because the Progressives believed that joining social science to government was the best way to assure general progress. In 1919, President Wilson used a more formal mechanism, the King-Crane Commission, to advise the U.S. government on the situation in the Middle East after the collapse of the Ottoman Empire. That commission did damage, too, but of an entirely different sort. Before long, the U.S. Congress got into the act, sponsoring commissions and investigations of its own. Probably the most famous of this historical variety from that era was the Nye Commission, which, after U.S. involvement in World War I, blamed arms manufacturers for the war and contributed to the isolationism of the interwar period.

Because commissions have a foot inside government but also a foot outside of it, they serve as a prime mixing bowl for governmental and non-governmental personnel and subcultures to engage each other. They produce a special kind of temporary revolving door. Federal commissions have long been major occasions for the joining of academia to the policy community, starting in the Progressive Era but continuing into the present. The aforementioned Kerner Commission Report took testimony and writings from dozens of prominent American social scientists. This was Camelot and the "best and the brightest" at its zenith.

Academics of a certain bent then and now also see federal commissions as an opportunity to play in policymaking. Of course, how well academics actually contribute to the solutions to problems, as opposed to making them worse, is a matter of ongoing debate. The first coming of what is called neoconservatism was not about foreign policy. It was about domestic policy, and especially about what the social science founders of neoconservatism believed were the pernicious and counterproductive effects of the programs of the Great Society. These original neoconservatives were appalled at the respect given and the recommendations offered up to the Kerner Commission by most of the social science experts eager to testify before it.[2]

It follows that proposals generated by federal commissions sometimes have unintended effects—perhaps because a commission's recommendations are heeded, as with the Kerner Commission, or because those recommendations are twisted. A good example concerns the U.S. Commission on National Security/21st Century, more commonly known as the Hart-Rudman Commission, which operated between 1999 and early 2001.

Cosponsored by the Secretary of Defense, the Speaker of the House, and the President, this commission was charged with a very broadly defined mission: (1) to examine the structure of the U.S. government's foreign and national security policy operations, (2) to determine if that structure was properly aligned with the developing post-Cold

---

2. You can read all about it in the pages of the now-defunct journal *The Public Interest*, the flagship of the original neoconservative movement.

War international environment, and (3) to recommend changes to the structure that would allow the government to promulgate and implement policy more effectively. The commission had a wide mandate, wide support in terms of its sponsorship, an unusually long term as federal commissions go, and 14 commissioners divided equally between Democrats and Republicans in order to take the edge of partisanship off its deliberations and potential impact.

The Hart-Rudman Commission had a professional staff, common for commissions of long duration, on which I served as a member. I worked for the executive director, who was the nexus between the commissioners and the staff. In the end, the recommendation for which the commission became best known was its proposal to establish a Department of Homeland Security, the first time that a new Executive Branch department had been proposed since the creation of the Department of Education during the Carter administration in the late 1970s. The commission pointed out that the three main border security agencies of the U.S. government—the Customs Service, the Border Patrol, and the Coast Guard—resided in three different executive departments (Customs was part of the Treasury Department; the Border Patrol, as well as the Immigration and Naturalization Service, was part of the Justice Department, and the Coast Guard was part of the Department of Transportation) and that this was a dysfunctional and accident-prone arrangement.

In terms of the U.S. national security structure, the commission's recommendations in this and other areas were by far the most thoroughgoing since the National Security Act of 1947. The commission based its proposal for a Homeland Security Department on an analysis of the rising threat of international terrorism and predictions of mass-casualty terrorist attacks on U.S. soil. The third and final report of the Hart-Rudman Commission came out in March 2001—just six months before the 9/11 attacks—and virtually no one took it seriously. The new Bush administration certainly didn't. It took the report and assigned it to an interagency group, chaired by Vice President Dick Cheney, which was scheduled to report out in October 1, 2001. We knew, however, from those few places in Washington where the commission's findings were taken seriously—Senator Joseph Lieberman's office, for example—that the Bush administration would not embrace its findings.

Then came the attacks of September 11, 2001. Suddenly, the commission's report became hot property. Politically, it was impossible for the Bush administration to duck the issue, and so it embraced the idea of a Homeland Security Department. However, it created that department in a way that spited nearly all the recommendations of the Hart-Rudman Commission's final report. The commission had called for an agency that had a light Washington footprint, that was not over-bureaucratized and over-centralized, and that pushed resources and responsibility out to first-responders. The Bush administration instead built the ponderous monstrosity of a bureaucracy we have today.

In politics it is frequently better to be lucky than to be right. Sometimes, however, one is right but unlucky. This occurs when the cue ball of absurdity strikes the other balls on the table, sending them off in all directions to no particular or obvious purpose. It happens a lot in government, regrettably, and it's what happened to the Homeland Security recommendations of the Hart-Rudman Commission. To sit and watch something like this happen from a privileged spot is truly an education in how politics work when all levels of government engage with one another. It makes one respect the time and trouble it actually takes to make any government function work properly; it also makes one skeptical by default of breathless proposals for change. It is extremely hard to get things done in government short of major crisis, and even major crisis does not guarantee that they get done well.

As may be easily surmised from the purposes of commission reports, the writing rules are basically the same for all varieties of the form, whether the writing comes from the federal government's Executive Branch, from the U.S. Congress, from a state legislature, or even from the county seat. The key is to be authoritative, and part of being authoritative involves being scientifically sound, objective, academic, and empirical, which can translate into dry, reportorial, tedious text. Being required to read such a document is no treat. It's not as bad as having to read the budget each year, which I am persuaded no one actually does. But it's bad. Yet commission reports have to be the way they are, at least to some extent. They have to appeal as a document, a historical archive before its time.

Not all commission reports end up as bad reading, however. The Hart-Rudman Commission reports were and still are good reading. (My bias here is manifest, since I wrote them, but my judgment is not necessarily off the mark.) So is the far better known 9/11 Commission Report, and there are good reasons for that.

One reason is that the executive director of the 9/11 Commission, Dr. Philip Zelikow, had read the Hart-Rudman Commission reports and saw that writings of this kind did not have to be the literary equivalent of going to the dentist. This is partly why he engaged Dr. Ernest May of Harvard University's history department to help write the 9/11 Commission report. Under the circumstances, the 9/11 Commission's report, the originators knew, would have a much, much larger audience in the United States and worldwide than any other federal commission report ever written. They wanted it to be a narrative with feeling and literary quality, and their models were the works of the popular historians Stephen Ambrose and David McCullough.

They got very close. The report was truly a great success, at least in analytical and literary terms, but, like the Hart-Rudman Commission experience, all did not turn out well with its recommendations. One of the 9/11 Commission's foci concerned the U.S. intelligence community. The commission recommended major reforms to the structure of the U.S. intelligence community, and the result of those recommendations is visible today in the Directorate of National Intelligence, which is the overarching structure that now stands above the Central Intelligence Agency. Like the Department of Homeland Security, the DNI is over-centralized and over-bureaucratized, yet underpowered in terms of budget control.

There are counter-examples of a sort. There have been commissions where consensus was reached and the written report turned out clear and of high quality, but the advice contained within it was wisely rejected by its target audience. The example that comes first and foremost to mind is the Iraq Study Group report of March 2006. This report made several recommendations regarding the war in Iraq and associated Middle East policy. President Bush rejected all of it, and decided on another course that became known as "the surge." In this case, the commission, though very prestigious and well spoken, turned out to be wrong and the President turned out to be right.

What all this shows is that no matter how well a commission report is written, and no matter how clearly its caveats against foolishness and error are stated, the American political system these days is capable of very quickly turning a silk purse into a sow's ear. So do not go into the task of writing commission reports unless you are prepared to have your work distorted and your heart broken. That said, it is at least "gainful employment." No salary check I ever got working on a commission report—and I was a consultant to the White House report on Hurricane Katrina, and on one other major multiyear effort, as well, concerning reform of what is known as the Interagency—ever bounced.

So how exactly does one set about writing these commission reports? The first thing to have firmly in mind is that the writer is not a free agent in such affairs, at least not entirely. We should also clarify what we mean by "the writer."

There are more writers involved in large bureaucratic efforts than the innocent-sounding term *writer* can possibly convey. There needs to be one chief writer, the person responsible ultimately for the way the report reads. Sometimes, depending on the particular commission, that chief writer can be the main drafter for the entire report. Usually, however, these things are so complex, require so much expert input, and have so many moving parts that a chief writer is mainly concerned with integrating, consolidating, and smoothing the style of writing that is the product of many different hands. Indeed, whatever else a chief writer of a commission report does, her main responsibility is making the final product appear to be the work of a single hand. There can only be one style sheet, one resonant style, and one dominant tone. It is simply not possible for more than one person to achieve those ends with any efficiency.

One way to think of the chief writer in a commission report, too, is less as an editor and more as an amanuensis. (If you do not understand that word, you know by now what you need to do. I will say no more.) As James Boswell was famously scribe to Samuel Johnson, the writer within a bureaucratic effort is scribe to many. First among these many are the commissioners, and first among the commissioners is the chair or cochairs, as the case may be.

So far so good; you take notes on what people say for future use. The problem is that commissioners may think that they have reached substantive consensus on aspects of the commission's mandate in their meetings when, in fact, looking at the transcript of their discussion, no such consensus actually exists at all. (Sometimes they think they disagree on a point when they really don't, but that is a less common problem.) Even at high levels of government, well-known people prefer to avoid frontal confrontations whenever possible, and politicians are particularly apt to do this, except on occasions where it benefits them to appear defiant or belligerent to useful constituencies. If you could just watch two Georgians, Republican Newt Gingrich and Democrat Andrew Young, in the same room with each other, you would understand. They are unfailingly polite to each other, they never argue or raise their voices, they go out of their way to praise one another, and they try to agree. Sometimes they genuinely persuade each other that they do agree—but they don't.

The result is that, as often as not, commissioners will leave a session believing that they are in accord. They all remember the heads nodding up and down; they never saw the dissent in the group, which does not nod at all most of the time. They also tend to believe that others agree with them unless they have firm evidence to the contrary. This is psychologically comforting, but it is often untrue and of no use at all in coming to agreement on difficult or sensitive points.

It follows that when the time comes to have this all written down, it is the writer who must identify the gaps, ambiguities, and contradictions among the commissioners and go to the executive director to ask what is to be done about them. Several possibilities open up at this point. The executive director may (1) defer to the cochairs, or pass the problem to them to work out; (2) call a small informal meeting to hash out points of disagreement among the major proponents of the different points of view; (3) find a way to simply eliminate discussion of points on which consensus cannot be found, if they are minor enough not to scuttle the whole effort; or (4) just tell the writer to do the best she can.

I have experienced all of these options, and I can tell you that this last one is by far the most fun and also the most dangerous. That is not an uncommon combination in life. And, for those of you who have been paying attention, you will note that it is not entirely different from eleventh-hour speechwriting on the road, when a principal's advisers cannot agree and he, or in my case she, turns to you and says, do the best you can.

Despite all these pitfalls, whoever holds the pen in such a circumstance has disproportionate power. It is one thing to bat about an idea in discussion; it is quite another to put it into writing. Only when a policy proposal is committed to writing does it become a truly externalized object for criticism and amendment. If the writer should happen to have a view on a contentious issue, he can often find a way to express that issue in such a way that will tilt it toward the outcome he favors. Sometimes sheer grace of expression can be persuasive in an environment in which the alternative is long hours of argument without any guarantee that one's point of view will prevail.

As already noted, it is one thing to get one's way in the writing of a commission report. It is another for a commission's ideas to be implemented as intended. To maximize the likelihood that a commission's efforts will not be in vain, all those involved in the endeavor must keep in mind five critical factors, or we can again call them rules, and these factors must be firmly understood by the writer(s) as well as by the commissioners, the executive director, and the rest of the staff.

RULE 1: A commission must propose new and actionable solutions for the problems that brought it into existence in the first place. If a commission proposes the same old tired recommendations spawned by earlier groups, it will be seen as having failed its mission and squandered its opportunity. Sometimes when commissions cannot agree among themselves, they fall back to lowest-common-denominator modes of thought. This is deadly. It is the job of the cochairs and the executive director to make sure this does not happen.

The chief writer can contribute to this effort by shaping language that forces reluctant commissioners in new and useful directions. Note, too, that in addition to final reports, the writer has influence over earlier drafts as well as study guide materials that the commissioners may request or find useful. All sorts of tactics are thus available to achieve the desired end. For example, a writer can listen carefully at formal sessions and can easily distill out thoughts and language that will resonate with given commissioners. If the writer wants those commissioners to buy into an idea or policy direction, he can improve his chances if he couches that idea or direction in language he knows will draw in certain commissioners.

RULE 2: New and actionable solutions must be tailored to the right level of analysis. As with writing a memo, it makes very little sense for a commission to recommend policy actions that the commission's sponsors are unable to implement. At the same time, it makes little sense to advocate policy actions so trivial that the sponsors need never have been involved.

Again, the chief writer can be instrumental in keeping the commission's report on the right level. Sometimes commissioners can get carried away with ideas, just as sometimes commissioners can be extraordinarily risk-averse. It is up to the writer, with the advice and consent of the executive director, to strike the right balance.

RULE 3: A commission must not wait until its recommendations are final and ready to be put before the sponsors and the country to start selling the ideas. Commission recommendations, if they are to stand a chance of implementation, need to be pre-briefed to core constituencies. If possible, new ideas should be co-conceived with core constituencies. It is important to identify and, to the extent possible, disarm opposition to what one wishes to do before one gets to the finish line, for by then it is often too late, especially if leaks of the commission's deliberations have fallen into the hands of its natural adversaries.

Again the chief writer can be of enormous value in this regard. In the first place, drafts of material need to be guarded carefully so that they do not fall into the hands of opposing camps. Writers also sometimes operate as memo drafters and speechwriters for commissioners and for the executive director as they pre-brief the commission's major proposals. It is important for the chief writer to be involved in all of these ancillary drafting tasks lest wires get crossed and contradictory language gets loosed into the corral. That needs to be prevented at all costs.

RULE 4: The prestige of the sponsor or sponsors, and the active engagement of a unified commission, must be mobilized behind the commission's aims. For this reason, it is better to work very hard at eliminating disagreements than it is to accept the idea of publishing reservations in the text of the report. The latter should be avoided whenever possible because it undermines the power that resides in the prestige of the commission's membership.

Yet again, a skillful chief writer can help avoid this kind of thing. There are times when it is better to create the appearance of agreement than to try but fail to actually produce it. Careful drafting and the benign uses of ambiguity can sometimes achieve this.

RULE 5: Take special pains to craft a masterful executive summary. Federal commission reports tend to be rather lengthy. Most violate the less-is-more rule in spades. Those with high-stakes engagement in the subject matter can be expected to read them in their entirety, but most people will not. Specifically, the press will only read the whole report if they are preternaturally interested in it, or if they are Walter Pincus of the *Washington Post*—who seems to like that sort of thing. The political circles in Washington will rely instead on the executive summary of the report. Since at least 50 times as many people will read the executive summary as will read the entire report, it is absolutely imperative that this executive summary be written at the very highest level of persuasive skill. Ten drafts are not enough; 20 or more are required.

For this reason, the executive summary cannot be left for last, or it is possible that time will run out before it can be properly crafted. The chief writer must have in mind from the very beginning of the drafting process what the executive summary needs to look like.

In addition to the executive summary, the final report of any federal commission will be accompanied by press releases and probably by statements at a press conference for the commission's rollout. It is common in commissions for everyone to be exhausted by the time the rollout rolls around, and to think of these marginal exercises as marginal—except that they are not marginal. The executive director and chief writer must be engaged in vetting, if not actually drafting, what gets said to the press assembled at a rollout, and what is put into a press release. (The press release, by the way, constitutes a minor persuasive art form of its own.) This language must not deviate from the core language of the commission report and its executive summary. If it does, then the deviations become the news story instead of the commission's core recommendations. That also is a disaster.

If a press release is a minor persuasive art form, what can be said about how to write one, whether in the context of a federal commission report or in any other context? Three things can be said. First, the thing must fit on one side of one piece of paper, or its electronic equivalent. So it must be very short and to the point. Second, it must clearly show the way to some office or person that can supply more information. And third, it must attract and not exhaust. A press release should whet the appetite, not satisfy it; open the door a crack, not all the way. It should promise typical journalists, who are the main targets of press releases at least here in Washington, that a spoon-fed story is in the offing, holding out the opportunity of making their job easier; but it must make them get off their duffs to get that story. If you give them too much in a press release, they'll never get off their barstools.

Federal commission reports, similar to the "white papers" of many other countries, are part of the fabric of American politics. These days there always seems to be at least one in the works, and often more than one. Most of them are not very important, and the consequences of their work often fall like a stone into a very deep well, never making a sound. A select few, however, are very consequential, for better or for worse. The writing that goes on within commissions combines just about every kind of persuasive writing there is. The staff writes essays and will occasionally write reviews of relevant literature. There are memos in abundance. Sometimes a writer will generate op-eds that will bear the signature of certain commissioners to advertise the commission's efforts during and after its tenure. A writer may draft speeches for commissioners or for the executive director. And then of course, there is the final report itself, with its executive summary.

Writing for a federal commission is a little like playing a hand of bridge in no-trump; tactics and expectations differ from the ordinary. (If you do not know how to play bridge, then you have something to look forward to during those hours in which you are no longer wasting your time watching television.) It is excellent practice, too, for any kind of writing a writer might wish to do later on, even as it reveals the American political process in all its glory. You could do a lot worse than getting some experience with a federal commission.

Recommended Reading

Mark M. Lowenthal, "Between the Lines of the Iraq Intelligence Estimate," *Washington Post*, February 11, 2007.

James A. Baker III & Lee H. Hamilton, cochairs, *The Iraq Study Group Report*, auth. ed. (New York: Vintage Books, 2006).

U.S. Commission on National Security/21st Century, "New World Coming," September 15, 1999.

Scan both the congressional (http://www.gpoaccess.gov/katrinareport/mainreport.pdf) and White House (http://library.stmarytx.edu/acadlib/edocs/katrinawh.pdf) "Katrina" reports.

Writing Exercise

Write the introduction to a hypothetical 2017 Federal Commission report on "The Great Pandemic of 2014." 1,500 words max.

11 BLOGS

As I indicated at the very start of this little book, a discussion of blogs did not make up part of my class syllabus when I taught political writing. As I also indicated, this idea belongs to the book's editor, but I do not resist it because I recognize the ubiquity of the blogosphere and the likelihood that it is here to stay.

I am not entirely at sea here, however, for I have dabbled myself in the form. For more than two years I have written episodically at thenewestdealer.blogspot.com. I do not put hyperlinks in that blog and I do not promote it, so it has a small readership. This does not concern me, because I use it just to get things off my chest that I suspect do not belong in any formal publication. In addition, I write in the blog space on the website of *The American Interest*: http://www.the-American-interest.com. Here, I am part of a group. I let the editors of that function insert hyperlinks and other references when they make sense. What I do not do is spend a lot of time reading blogs (except those of my colleagues on the website of my own magazine), so I am admittedly less expert at this form of persuasive writing than I am in the more traditional forms.

There is a reason for this. While there are some truly wonderful, nearly miraculous, aspects of the information technology revolution, there are also, in my view as well as that of others, several significant downsides. This is not the place to provide a full analysis of what remains a highly controversial issue; many entire books and essays by the score appear on this subject every year.[1] Suffice it to say that blogs are of a piece with the subculture of the internet-driven cybernetic

---

1. The first significant critique of the internet-driven world in which we live today—still worth reading more than 18 years after its original publication—is Sven Birkerts, *The Gutenberg Elegies: The Fate of Reading in an Electronic Age* (New York: Faber & Faber, 1994). Birkerts's reflections on his own work may be found in "Refuse It," *The American Interest* (July–August 2009).

world; they are incomprehensible except as a part of it. As a result, blogs benefit from the positive side of that new world and suffer from its negative sides.

E ven at the risk of being seen as a curmudgeon, I must review briefly what seems to me to be the negative side. The internet and the blogosphere have no filters. They represent the democratization of both opinion and access to information, but they are misleading potentially to those whose educations have failed to provide them with sufficient context to judge and understand what is before them on the screen. There is an old adage that a little bit of knowledge can be a dangerous thing, and it is true. The internet and the blogosphere can make it seem like a person has learned a lot in a very short time, and hence has a right to broadcast his opinion about assorted subjects. He does have a right and that right must be preserved; but that doesn't mean he is wise to exercise it. Information is not the same as knowledge. Information is just data; knowledge is the systematic absorption of information into a framework defined by a purpose. The concept is well summarized by a remark once made by the British anthropologist Mary Douglas: "Information is not going to rub off on someone who is never going to use it."[2]

Without such a purposeful framework, data can overflow to such an extent that it paralyzes the recipient. That is one of the preeminent dangers of the internet and the blogosphere; so much comes at us so fast that we are unable to process what it all means. We may thus be tempted to latch onto superficial islands of coherence we may find and mistake them for actual understanding.

A second negative aspect concerns the general collapse of standards. Where there is no filter and where the market does not exact any penalty for substandard product, there is no way to enforce standards of evidence, rules of logic, or literary disciplines such as punctuation or grammar. As a result, when people read blogs more than any other form of writing, they tend to forget—if they ever learned in the first place—what those standards, rules, and disciplines are. If they are young people who never learned better in the first place, then they have no neutral third point from which to judge what they are seeing. This

---

2. Mary Douglas, "Governability: A Question of Culture," *Millennium: Journal of International Studies,* 22, no. 3 (December 1993).

means that their effort to find an internal standard of excellence, should such an effort ever be undertaken, is unlikely to be aided by reading blogs, especially if that is what someone mainly reads.

Consider, for example, what happens to "less is more" in a world suffused with blogs. We know that the refinement of language, whether we are refining our own language or editing the language of others, almost invariably consists of boiling down longer texts into tighter and more elegant shorter ones. In the world of print culture, a piece that is short but of high quality indicates that a great deal of work has been put into it. It indicates that principles of exclusion have been applied. But blogs, which are mostly short, indicate nothing of the sort most of the time. They are not distillations of genuine thinking but first impressions blurted out mostly unrefined. They reward spontaneity, emotion, and stark naked opinion, not patience, reason, and learning. They privilege the new over the true, the stylish over the substantive, self-expression over intersubjectivity, and the easy over the earned. They exude a form of rhetoric Aristotle would have hated, and a debased form of "knowledge" Socrates warned against.

Serious people used to be ashamed of letting loose such unrefined material into the public domain, but that was when people were still capable of feeling shame. We now live in a no-fault world wherein any inkling of shame is inverted into contempt aimed toward the source of that inkling. As Lynne Truss has put it,

> Shamelessness is not only a highly regarded modern attribute, but the *sine qua non* of most successful TV and entertainment formats, which compete to push shamelessness to ever further limits.[3]

Shamelessness actually makes sense in the blogosphere for another reason, which is that people tend to read mostly self-reinforcing materials. Years ago, some optimists predicted that the democratization and proliferation of opinion would contribute positively to intellectual and policy debates of all sorts. There would be more different views out there and they would be much easier to access, it was declared to great hopes; everyone would then develop a better sense of possibilities, leading ultimately to a greater willingness to see and understand other points of view and thus to compromise. Nothing of the sort has

---

3. Lynne Truss, *Talk to the Hand* (New York: Gotham Books, 2005), p. 132.

happened. Instead, most people shore up their natural uncertainty about complicated issues by reading other people who already agree with them, or with whom they already agree—it amounts to more or less the same thing. We now have a massive electronic form of niche groupthink.

Niche groupthink makes it much easier to say truly stupid things in blogs and not get called on them, because most of your readers are sympathetic to your cause. Those who are not, and especially those who like to engage in ad hominem internet insults as a kind of hobby or game, are not really interested in joining an argument; their motives are more disparaging than anything else. Violations of Sidney Hook's maxim, that one should address someone's argument before disparaging his motives, are multiplying like cockroaches all over our computers.

Some people actually think that virtual communities exist thanks to the internet and the blogosphere. If they do, it depends on how one understands the term community. Some people think that these communities are real, and to some extent they are. Some argue that the internet is actually making people more social, not less. New social networking applications, which amount to exchanges of miniblogs in some respects, are "augmenting our people skills" (so to speak) and creating new possibilities for total strangers to share ideas and experiences. Indeed, we can now "friend"—used as a verb—any number of people we have never met and are never likely to meet.

To my mind, this is all a large heap of rubbish. In the first place, it is an obscene banalization of friendship to use the verb "to friend" in this sense, or in any sense at all. Real friendships are earned, and they are therefore actually worth something to those involved. The groups that people belong to by virtue of the fact that they follow certain clusters of blogs, and engage in other ways on the internet, are hardly real in the sense that actual groups are real. Whatever information is zooming around in hyperspace we can choose to ignore if we like. We control our cyberspace, and we become accustomed to thinking that, because we control our own cyberspace, we can control our space in public. A screen-bound life is not good training for actual human relationships, and it probably accounts at least in part for the rise of the unspeakably rude behavior we now witness regularly in public places. So self-absorbed and asocial have many people become, that they do not recognize the existence of other people if those other people are not at the moment instrumentally useful to them. Again, Lynne Truss:

We edit the world; we select from menus; we pick and choose; our social "group" focuses on us and disintegrates without us. This makes it
rather confusing for us when we step outdoors and discover that other
people's behaviour can't be deleted with a simple one-stroke command
or dragged to the trash icon.[4]

Then there is the matter of attention spans. Those inured to the
internet and to the blogosphere operate at high speeds but tend to
absorb only small bits, or bytes, of impressions at any one time. They
tend to become bored with longer pieces of writing far more than
they used to, to the point where they find themselves literally unable
to finish them. It was the realization that his own attention span was
shrinking dramatically that sent Nicholas Carr to research what information technology might be doing to the human brain. He published
his conclusions in *The Shallows*.[5] There is rapidly mounting evidence
that the internet-driven world of which blogs are part does rewire the
human brain, particularly the brains of children.[6] There is evidence,
too, that the way we use our eyes affects our endocrine system, so that
when people speak metaphorically of BlackBerry or iPhone addiction,
they tend not to realize that this is no metaphor. The addiction is real,
except that we don't typically use that term to refer to an addiction
to experience as opposed to substances. So it becomes a joke. Genuine
scientific experts on addiction, however, know better, and they are
not laughing.

If you don't believe this, ask yourself how many times a day you check
your e-mail. Nearly all computers and some phones have built in them
some indicator of when an e-mail is received. On mine, a little blue box
shows up in the lower right corner, accompanied by a cute little "ding."
If you habitually stop what you are doing in order to check e-mail,
assuming that you are not doing this at work because you know your
boss is telling you something you need to know *now*, you are engaged
in segmenting your time into ever-smaller pieces. If you automatically
respond to the electronic bells and whistles alerting you that you have

---

4. Truss, *Talk to the Hand*, p. 83.
5. Nicholas Carr, *The Shallows: What the Internet Is Doing to Our Brains* (New
York: W.W. Norton, 2010). See also the review by Sven Birkerts, "You Are What
You Click," *The American Interest* (September–October 2010).
6. By all means, see Maryanne Wolf, *Proust and the Squid: The Story and Science of
the Reading Brain* (New York: Harper, 2007).

a new message, you are in effect engaging in a classical conditioning experiment, Pavlovian style—except that *you are the dog*. The technology is harvesting you, and it will continue to do so if you let it.

Just one final curmudgeonly observation: When your useful time is segmented into ever-smaller parts, it becomes more difficult to maintain a logical train of thought. You essentially import symptoms of attention deficit disorder. If you render yourself incapable of reading long essays, let alone serious books, you will rob yourself of the opportunity to train your mind to actually think. Consider this recent observation from Henry Kissinger:

> A book is a large intellectual construction; you can't hold it all in mind easily or at once. You have to struggle mentally to internalize it. Now there is no need to internalize because each fact can instantly be called up again on the computer. There is no context, no motive. Information is not knowledge. People are not readers but researchers, they float on the surface. . . . This new thinking erases context. It disaggregates everything. All this makes strategic thinking about world order nearly impossible to achieve.[7]

Kissinger made this extemporaneous comment in the context of thinking about international politics, but the observation goes for thinking about any difficult topic. If you can't distinguish information from knowledge, and you can't distinguish knowledge from wisdom, it means you cannot think. If the internet-driven world in which we live today obscures these distinctions, then it is not helping its users to think. It is imbecilizing them instead.

You can stop cringing now. Although there is a lot more that I could say, even to the point of lathering myself into a full-fledged leather-lunged rant, I am finished with previewing the dark side of our internet-driven world. I will now light the light of the bright side.

There is no question that the existence of the blogosphere has encouraged large numbers of people to express themselves, to think, to engage, and to overcome their inhibitions. This is all to the good. There

---

7. Kissinger's comment was captured and is quoted in Charles Hill, *Grand Strategies: Literature, Statecraft and World Order* (New Haven: Yale University Press, 2010), p. 298.

are lots of people in the blogosphere who are quite thoughtful, quite talented, and quite good writers. It is possible that most of these people would never have surfaced had it not been for the blogosphere. There are brilliant bloggers who are, for example, stay-at-home parents in their thirties raising three children who just don't have time to go at rhetoric and polemics the old-fashioned way. There are young people, not yet ready for professional life, who have truly novel things to say that are worth careful attention. We can now have conversations across national borders and cultures far more easily than before, and that is a great benefit to those willing to engage in them.

It almost goes without saying that fact-finding and fact-checking have become far more efficient thanks to the internet, so long as the finder or checker is educated enough to use the resources at hand intelligently. While an investment of labor is still necessary to truly master any subject, and while the speed of cyberspace can make it all seem too easy for one's own good, it is hard to see what good purpose is served by having to spend half an hour looking up standard data as opposed to spending three minutes acquiring the same information online. Of course, blogs make very good use of this advantage.

Similarly, it is so obvious that it is easy to miss the point that there are huge time and cost advantages to the blogosphere as compared to more traditional ways of getting thought transformed into forms of writing. What used to take weeks, if not months, to make it from drafts into finished publications now takes literally hours. What used to cost judicious readers dozens of dollars is now virtually free. All else equal, this has to be counted a good thing.[8]

The overarching point is that all of the pitfalls of the blogosphere can be overcome with a diligent application of caution. For example, blogs do not have to be short and superficial. On the website of *The American Interest*, Walter Russell Mead, Francis Fukuyama, and Peter Berger regularly write essays of 3,000 to 5,000 words, and judging by the number and quality of the comments they attract, they have plenty of readers. Ross Douthat of the *New York Times* online is a master at

---

8. The problem, of course, is that all else is never equal. We know that banks, insurance companies, and government agencies at all levels, to name only three types of large organizations out of many hundreds, now have at their disposal the fastest information processing technologies in the history of the world. So why is it that many standard clerical operations take longer than ever? I will leave you to ponder . . .

thinking in short, concise paragraphs, making him a rare blogger who gives up nothing for all the snares of the medium.

You do not have to become a slave to your smartphone. You do not have to indulge the superficial, the emotional, the ad hominem, and the shameless. You do not have to allow your attention span to shrivel up, and to rush about madly from trivia to trivia. You do not have to fall into niche groupthink. You do not have to let technology colonize your personality and turn you into a walking example of rudeness. But these dire conditions are the default drive of those who become swallowed by their own gadgets. So it will take an effort on your part to avoid such a fate. You will have to remain critically conscious of how information technology affects you before it affects you in ways that short-circuit your capacity for critical consciousness.

How might you protect yourself? There are lots of ways open to you. You can get in the habit of taking long walks in the woods. You can take long-distance bicycle rides; nothing slows you down, in the good sense, like biking from, say, Philadelphia to Portland, Maine. You can always be reading good fiction, as I have already suggested, and you can do it with a real book in your hand rather than a Kindle. You can do yoga or meditate on a regular basis, and getting regular exercise actually helps, too—as long as you are not wired up when you do it!

My most trusted method for preventing others from shaping my mind for me is to unplug myself completely from the cyberworld 25 hours a week, every week at a set time. This refreshes my soul. It is common to the point of chic nowadays to disparage Sabbatarian customs as hopelessly outdated. Actually, such observances are probably more important than ever.

If for one reason or another you intend to write a blog, you will do so no doubt with certain purposes in mind. Those purposes may shape your standards of writing to one degree or another, for your purposes will presuppose your main intended audience. As a general rule, though, the strategy of essay writing, presented in Chapter 4, should guide you in the writing of blogs. Insofar as possible, resist the emotionalism, the present orientation, and the superficialities of standard blog discourse. There is no rule promulgated from on high that says blogs must always be what they usually are today. They are a new form of rhetoric, a new kind of polemic, and so they are particularly malleable to human design. Perhaps if enough people insist on standards of evidence, rules of logic, and rigorous literary discipline, the genre will mature. One can at least hope so.

Recommended Reading

Go to www.the-american-interest.com and read the blogs there; then follow the links to other blogs. Then take a long walk in the woods, trying to remember and think about what you read. Note when, or if, you run out of material.

Writing Exercise

Go through today's *New York Times*, *Washington Post*, or *Wall Street Journal* and write a blog entry of no longer than 250 words (with hyperlinks), expressing your take on the day's news.

12 A PHILOSOPHY OF EDITING

The words *editing* and *editor* are two of the most plastic words in the English language. These words can refer to everything from routine administrative tasks to highly philosophical ones. It is impossible to know what either word really means except from context. But one thing is very clear: All good writers do a great deal of editing on their own drafts, so that writing and editing are not as distinct as one might think.

Be that as it may, not all good writers make good editors, and not all good editors are good writers. Some writers are tone deaf to other people's styles. When they edit other people's works, they are prone to try to make them sound like their own. Individual styles of writing may be compared to fingerprints or snowflakes; in a sense they are all the same, even though, as everyone knows, they are all different. By the same token, some very good editors never manage to find their own muse. Possibly this is because they lack a certain passion. As the great American novelist F. Scott Fitzgerald once said, "You don't write because you want to say something, you write because you've got something to say." Fitzgerald spoke in the context of fiction, of course, but his remark, if anything, goes double for rhetoric and polemic.

So while writing and editing are different, in practice they intermingle. It is very hard even for excellent writers to edit themselves. Oftentimes, they have a forest-and-trees problem, by which I mean that they are so emotionally engaged in their writing projects that they cannot see clearly the discipline needed to control the final product. They cannot readily enforce their principles of exclusion. It is often the case that the sentences, and especially the quips, wit, and humor that an author likes best, are precisely the sentences a skilled editor should summarily delete. It is possible to have too much fun with one's own writing. A good rule of thumb is to check the ratio of your adjectives and adverbs to your nouns and to compare them to a piece of writing that you know to be excellent. You will discover most of the time that you need to cull your modifiers by a significant percentage.

So everyone needs an editor, and it is almost a law of literary nature that mature and excellent writers are grateful to their editors, while novices complain at the least movement of a comma, thinking their every word spun of pure gold. I am using the words *editor* and *editing* here in the elevated tense. But that begs the question of how many meanings these words can have. So let us quickly march through the basic typology.

There are five different and overlapping forms of editing. The first is *proofreading or technical editing*. This kind of editing looks for mistakes of all sorts and applies any publication's or discipline's style guide to the text. As we noted in Chapter 2, not every rule of writing is hard and fast. Some judgments are mere convention; others are matters of taste. The point is to be consistent, and that is what a style guide does: It takes the guesswork out of proofreading and technical editing.

The second kind of editing is *style editing*, sometimes called *line editing*. Style editing is designed to make a piece of writing flow smoothly. It looks for all of the errors noted in Chapters 2 and 3, and it fixes them. So it is attentive to rhythm and cadence. It is attentive to the consistent and sensible use of verb tenses. It ruthlessly turns around passive voice sentences and sends all examples of the documentary tense to the wall. Above all, competent line editing enforces the less-is-more edict with a vengeance.

Some writers are quite practiced at keeping their logic straight and their arguments sound. Some are also adequate or better at matters of structure, so that the argument in any piece of writing they proffer lays out in the right order. Certain writers are fine at all of this but lack a sense of style. It is quite remarkable how an essay, or any other piece of persuasive writing, can be transformed at this level. An excellent line editor is worth her weight in gold. This skill has sometimes been characterized as leatherwork, by which is meant the ability to turn a sow's ear into a silk purse.

The third kind of editing is *structural editing*, sometimes called *deep editing* or content editing or developmental editing—there are several acceptable terms for it. If line editing focuses on the text sentence by sentence, deep editing is more concerned with the paragraph by paragraph and section by section architecture of a piece of writing. There are some authors whose style is most admirable, but whose facility with logical presentation is not. Structural editing is most often forced into action by an author's failure to identify principles of exclusion. It is also required when the balance between argument and evidence is off kilter. One does not, or at any rate should not, adduce seven sources for a minor point and only one for a major pillar of an argument, but authors do this from time to time. Overkill in elaborating small points is often a function of the fact that the author simply knows all these things and wishes the reader to admire him for that knowledge. But this is foolish, especially in political writing. One should never allow ego to trump purpose. When authors forget this fundamental rule, it is an editor's duty to remind them of it.

Structural editing can be tricky when the editor is dealing with a subject on which he is not expert. There are times when an editor can see that a piece of writing is either unintelligible or unpersuasive or both, but may not know enough about the subject matter to put it right. In such cases, essays often enter what is known as the query stage. If the editor cannot fix what he senses is wrong, he can ask the author questions within the text that force clarification. Sometimes an editor may seek help from another expert in the field. This is one purpose served by editorial advisory boards. All journals and magazines have one, and so do most newspapers and publishing houses.

Editing thus involves skill not just at manipulating text, but also skill in the care and feeding of sometimes temperamental expert authors. In these queries, an editor must be clear and uncompromising, but always polite and even deferential. Structural editing can be an iterative process, therefore. A text may go back and forth between editor and author many times before the internal standards of excellence have been met for both parties. This can be very time-consuming, and it can ruffle feathers. It can, as well, involve what might be called manipulation as the editor tries to get the author to not just see things his way, but to do them his way.

Editors also lie to authors about deadlines, word length, and sometimes the size of their payment. Some need to do this on a regular basis, not just because they enjoy it, but because it is necessary. If you tell an author that she has until December 4 to hand in her work, she will hand it in on December 14 much of the time. That is why if your real deadline is December 14, you tell the author December 4. That is a lie, of course. If you tell an author that she has 5,000 words to use, she will likely hand in 6,000. Therefore, if your real length parameter is 6,000 words, you will tell her 5,000. In other words, an editor will lie to build in a buffer against the typical foibles exhibited by writers. This constant need for manipulation and lying is the reason that the author, journalist, and Hollywood insider Gene Fowler once said, "Every editor should have a pimp for a brother, so he has someone to look up to."[1]

Let us return to the various types of editing, picking up on the fourth kind, *critical editing*. Editing of this sort is of a specific and esoteric nature. It has to do with revising and reintroducing an older work written by someone else. One might think at first blush that this has nothing to do with rhetoric or polemic, and sometimes it doesn't. But it can and often does. To take one example, there was a fascinating and hard-to-categorize American political and social observer named William Graham Sumner who taught at Yale University for decades in the second part of the nineteenth century. More recently, he has been rediscovered and gathered to the bosom of libertarians. One such organization created a compendium of his work, which for the most part is an honest recreation of his thinking, but which leans, along with its introduction by the editor, just a bit toward a particular aspect of Sumner's thought.[2] Nonlibertarians who want to read Sumner today are likely to pick up this volume because it is a very economical and time-saving way to crack the literature. But such readers may be misled inadvertently by the way this volume was put together—in this case, less by sins of commission than by those of omission.

There are also multiple editions of the works of Alexis de Tocqueville, Karl Marx, Theodor Herzl, and countless others who function as historical avatars for modern-day admirers or critics. Every one of these editions is a critical edition in one way or another, and each carries a capacity to influence readers in ways that the editor, but not the original author, can to some extent determine.

Critical editions that are also translations are even more subject to manipulation, and should be read, therefore, with even greater care. Nowhere is the historical impact of critical editing greater than in the remote editing of key religious texts. For stellar examples, one need look no further than the creation of the Septuagint—the first Greek-language version of the Hebrew Bible—or the translation of the original Christian Gospels from Aramaic into Greek.

---

1. As quoted in G.W. Mank's *Hollywood's Hellfire Club* (Port Townsend, WA: Feral House, 2007).

2. I have in mind Robert C. Bannister, ed., *On Liberty, Society, and Politics: The Essential Essays of William Graham Sumner* (Indianapolis: Liberty Fund, 1992).

The fifth and final kind of editing to be noted is *conceptual editing*. Conceptual editing is about conceiving and managing the writing of others, either as individuals or as ensembles of individuals. Journal and magazine editors fall into this category. They are impresarios of the intellect. Most intellectually serious and influential journals and magazines, at least in the United States and the Western world generally, are born issue by issue in the mind of an editor. An editor will fix on the subjects she thinks will be most important at the time of publication, be that a week, a month, or three months in advance, and she will solicit essays and reviews of various shapes and descriptions to make that happen. Depending on her purposes, she will conceive individual issues as having certain balances—of length, of tone, of topic, and of political perspective. She will also keep in mind such balances not only within a given issue, but within all the issues of a given publication as they are born over time.[3]

It should now be clear to you that there exists a horizon-to-horizon arc of difference between a technical editor and a conceptual editor. Despite all these differences, though, there are some guidelines applicable to all, or nearly all, forms of editing.

The first of these guidelines is a version of the Goldilocks problem that we have come to know and admire. The editor should not do too little, for that is laziness and leaves errors unredressed. But an editor should not do too much either. This is the hardest and most constant dilemma facing conscientious editors. The rule of thumb in taking on any given sentence or paragraph is that what an editor does to it should make it better, not worse. At the same time, there are ways of making sense differently that are neither better nor worse. Just as writers need to vary their sentence structures and lengths, sometimes editors fall into stale patterns in their editing. Sometimes they will change sentences so that they read their way rather than a better way. Editors should avoid this trap, which amounts to another form of laziness.

Sometimes an editor can make a case that a changed sentence or paragraph is at least a little better than the original, but he should leave it alone anyway. Those times are defined by an editing task that

---

3. You can get a feel for this process in an obituary: Eric Pace, "William Shawn, 85, Is Dead; *New Yorker's* Gentle Despot," *New York Times*, December 9, 1992.

literally leaves no sentence unmolested. Editors develop an intuition about just how much tampering most writers will tolerate. If an editor has rewritten six out of ten sentences in a two-paragraph stretch, he should not rewrite the seventh if the positive difference produced would be marginal. In other words, there is a role for tact in editing.

The second guideline is very clear: Editing is not arguing with an author over matters of substance. An editor is a little bit like a lawyer or speechwriter. The job is to make the principal sound as good and as persuasive as possible. It doesn't matter if the editor is of a different view. Obviously, this advice is subject to interpretation. An editor might wish to change a subsidiary element of an argument in order to make the overall argument more logical and hence more persuasive. One simply has to use one's judgment in assessing what the author will and will not allow. As in speechwriting, an editor has to know his principal. If one is editing an author for the first time, he may be reduced to guessing. But it is not uncommon for editors and authors to work together on more than one occasion, and one can get to know the limits of particular writers. One can also get to know their weaknesses, and writers can get to know editors' strengths. In this sense, a long-term relationship between an editor and writer comes in some ways to resemble a correspondence.

It is worth pointing out here that a magazine is different from a book. When one is editing a book, that book is the author's—hook, line, and sinker. When in doubt, the author is right. Even when not in doubt, often the author is still right. But when one is editing an essay that will go within a magazine bearing the work of many others, that essay, if it is to be part of a composite with the right balances, belongs at least to some degree also to the editor. The editor is responsible for the overall finished product of which each individual essay or review is a part. Thus, the editor has a right to expect that individual authors will recognize this reality and defer appropriately. Of course, this does not always happen. This is why some authors end up writing for a particular magazine or journal just once.

Above all, skillful editing manages to keep the voice, and the music, of others intact. There is always a way to fix what needs to be fixed in a piece of writing without robbing the author of his individuality. In this sense, it is useful to think of the editing process as a merging of minds. It is again like speechwriting in a way, except that whereas speechwriting is an out-of-body experience for the speechwriter, editing is more like a closely performed duet.

That is not all that skillful editors, at least conceptual editors, need to do to be successful. Ideally, they need the support of a generous and thoughtful publisher, someone who will leave them alone editorially and take care of the business end of things effectively. It is very hard for editors to do creative work effectively while spending half their time trying to raise money. It is also very hard to edit effectively if you are not alone. Coeditorships are sometimes suggested by organizations or publishers. They are usually a very bad idea. Even if two people start out as like-minded friends, copublishing a journal or magazine is likely to end their friendship in a hurry.

Another problem for conceptual editors is inspiration fatigue. Everybody has ups and downs, and sometimes the creative muse takes an extended vacation. This, again, is where editorial advisory boards come in. Members of the board can supply inspiration as well as specific suggestions as to topics and authors. Sometimes editors don't want to hear these things when they have in mind a full plate of their own aspirations, but they need to hear them all the same.

The best protection against inspiration fatigue is to read widely and variously. This is not just so that an editor knows what other magazines and journals are doing, although that is certainly important. It is also to stimulate the imagination. You may recall that early in this little volume I advised you as budding intellects and professionals to read in balance between depth and breadth. The same applies to editors, and for more or less the same reasons.

Finally, editors need to be both quick and slow. They need to be quick to seize opportunities, and slow to be satisfied in seeing them through to fruition. Changes in media technology and habits in recent decades have quickened the news cycle. The editor of the daily or weekly will soon be roadkill if he does not figure a way to shove a publication into that news cycle. The editor of a bimonthly or a quarterly, on the other hand, is a fool to chase headlines, but that editor is confronted with an even more daunting task: seeing around the curve of the future to know what people will want to read three or six or nine months from now. There is nothing wrong with acting on a hunch. To some extent, editors are paid to act on their hunches. But some things cannot be rushed, nor should they be. The admonition to be patient is all well and good, and no one can argue with it. But the admonition does not tell you *when* to be patient. Alas, crossing this particular river from cleverness to wisdom is something we must figure out on our own.

Recommended Reading

Blake Morrison, "Black Day for the Blue Pencil," *The Guardian*, August 6, 2005.

Eric Pace, "William Shawn, 85, Is Dead; New Yorker's Gentle Despot," *New York Times*, December 9, 1992.

Lynne Truss, *Eats, Shoots & Leaves* (New York: Gotham, 2004), with Louis Menand, "Bad Comma," *The New Yorker*, June 28, 2004.

Writing Exercise

This is your final writing exercise. Assemble and edit everything you have written in conjunction with reading and studying this book, then get a colleague or buddy—if you have been fortunate enough to find such a colleague, as suggested in the introduction—to edit it for you. You, please, do the same for that person. Then vet and integrate your buddy's suggestions into your work.

Next, compose an introduction and an epilogue for the result. Get a good night's sleep, awake the next day, and go outside if the weather permits; then—slowly, carefully, and self-critically—read what you've written.

Finally, sigh and vow to do better the next time you write anything of substance and length, and the time after that, and the time after that, until you finally find and recognize as earned your internal standard of excellence. You will then have conquered your mountain. It will feel really, really great.

SOME PARTING WORDS

Some people like to say that it's a dog-eat-dog world. It most certainly is not. I, for one, have never met a dog that had any intention of eating another dog. No one ever says that it's a fish-eat-fish world, although fish eat other fish all the time. We live in a curious society, it seems, one that makes a practice of saying things that are not so and ignoring things that are, so much so that one wonders sometimes whatever will become of it.

Similarly, some people are also very fond of saying about the competitive character of all life that one must either eat or be eaten. (Maybe they know something about fish after all.) Perhaps this used to be true a very long time ago, when our proto-human ancestors roamed about in fear of being the prey of large beasts. What is true now, however, and what this book has been about, is that one must either persuade or be persuaded. Even if you have no intention of having anything to do with politics in your lifetime, and therefore have determined that you need no instruction on how to write persuasively, you will nevertheless be ever a target of certain others who will be doing their best to persuade you of one thing or another. Not taking the offense in the great and sometimes even noble game of politics still leaves you with the obligations of self-defense against those who will.

Chances are, however, that you would not have read to the end of this little book if the notion of engaging in politics had never occurred to you. You might as well admit it: You want the advantage of being able to persuade others more adeptly than they are likely to be able to persuade you. Good for you. John Wayne once said, supposedly, that "life is hard, and it's harder if you're stupid." I would rephrase that for our purposes just a bit: Life is hard, and it's harder if you're inarticulate and gullible. I am not in a position to help you much with the latter vulnerability, but I hope this book has helped you more than a little with the former one.

You may never have need of many of the chapters in this book. You may never have anything to do with writing commission reports, for example. You may never have to write a eulogy text. You may even live in a world in which footnotes have become obsolete. (Heaven forfend!) But even if you have no need for certain chapters, the instructions within them have general relevance for the task of learning to write persuasively. Let us then sum up the essence of what may be learned here, even from chapters you might have skipped.

By now you will have taken into your own reservoir of knowledge a fundamental truth repeated many times in these pages: You must know your purpose. Recall Lewis Carroll's assertion that "if you don't know where you're going, most any road will take you there." He was right (as well as characteristically witty), and your name does not have to be Alice to appreciate the power of the insight. To know your purpose within any given writing project, however, you must also know your audience. You must always do whatever it is you wish to do *to* someone through your words. To have a purpose in political writing amounts to a transitive verb; no purpose can exist outside of its target, any more than an arrow can really be said to fly straight if it is not aiming at anything in particular.

If this is all you remember from reading this book, it will have done you much good. But I daresay there are two other lessons to keep close. The first of these is that emotion and reason mingle always in every aspect of human culture, not least politics. You may have reason on your side in a given argument, but reason alone will not always avail in the heat of debate. You must make reason appealing; you must make words that are standing still get up and dance to the rhythm of hearts and souls. You must be a composer of the intellect if you want to succeed.

The second of these lessons is that there is very little in political life that does not carry with it a moral consequence. Even the "how" questions of politics are not for the engineers and budgeteers alone; how much more so is this the case for the "why" questions! You will not be successful in politics unless your success truly serves what is right and good, so, as I told you at the very beginning, you must spare no effort to learn what these are, not from someone else telling you so, but by gleaning truth from your own experience. The key to that process is to never allow cynicism to muddy your sense of right and wrong. As Oscar Wilde famously said, a cynic is someone "who knows the price of everything and the value of nothing." To really succeed in politics, you must come to understand that true value has no price. Virtue cannot be bought, only earned.

Now be off with you; your mountain awaits.

INDEX

Italic page references indicate boxed text.

ABOUT THE AUTHOR

Dr. Adam Garfinkle is founding editor of *The American Interest*. He served from 2003 to 2005 as principal speechwriter to the U.S. Secretary of State (S/P, Policy Planning). Prior to that, he was editor of *The National Interest*. He has held appointments as professorial lecturer in American foreign policy at the School for Advanced International Studies (SAIS) at Johns Hopkins University. He has also taught at the University of Pennsylvania, Haverford College, and other institutions of higher learning.

Dr. Garfinkle served as a member of the National Security Study Group (as chief writer) of the U.S. Commission on National Security/21st Century (the Hart-Rudman Commission), and as an aide to Senator Henry M. Jackson (D-WA). His essays have been published in many magazines, journals, and newspapers, and he has appeared on national and international media. Dr. Garfinkle is the recipient of awards and grants from the U.S. Department of State, the Fulbright Fellowship Program, the American Academy in Berlin, the German Marshall Fund, the United States Institute of Peace, and the Moshe Dayan Center for the Study of Middle Eastern and African Affairs (Tel Aviv University).

Dr. Garfinkle received his Ph.D. in international relations from the University of Pennsylvania in 1979. He is married and has three children. He resides in Potomac, Maryland.